D1355009

The 1988 Michael J. McGivney Lectures
of the John Paul II Institute for Studies
on Marriage and Family

MORAL ABSOLUTES

Tradition, Revision, and Truth

John Finnis

The Catholic University of America Press
Washington, D.C.

The paper used in this publication meets the minimum requirements of American
National Standards for Information Science—Permanence of Paper for Printed
Library materials. ANSI Z39.48-1984.

∞

LIBRARY OF CONGRESS CATALOGING-IN-PUBLICATION DATA
Finnis, John.
  Moral absolutes: tradition, revision, and truth / John Finnis.
      p. cm.—(The Michael J. McGivney lectures of the John Paul II Institute
for Studies on Marriage and Family; 1988)
  Includes bibliographical references and index.
  ISBN 0-8132-0744-4 (alk. paper).—ISBN 0-8132-0745-2 (pbk.: alk. paper)
    1. Christian ethics—Catholic authors. 2. Ethical relativism—Controversial
literature. 3. Catholic Church—Doctrines.
  I. Title. II. Series.
BJ1249.F54 1991
241' .042—dc20   90-26434

Contents

Foreword

These are the four Michael J. McGivney Lectures, given at the Pontifical John Paul II Institute for Studies on Marriage and Family, Washington, D.C., in September 1988, as the first in a series of annual public lectures to be sponsored by that institute and by the charitable foundation the Knights of Columbus, which Fr. McGivney initiated in 1882. The lectures were delivered in the Dominican House of Studies in Washington, whose true hospitality I enjoyed over a number of weeks. The annotations which I have added here and there, but nowhere exhaustively, are a scant measure of the service rendered by the house's fine library.

The lectures leave much unsaid. They attempt no more than an overview of a much debated and most important question of faith and morals, and an outline of some grounds for thinking it reasonable to propose and accept a definite answer.

21 September 1990

CHAPTER I

Foundations

1. Exceptionless moral norms: few but strategic

The foundations of Christian moral doctrine are being tested as never before.

Dissension is well known. But does it go beyond rather marginal questions about the number and precise identity of the true moral absolutes? Does it challenge the very possibility of true moral absolutes? Does it go to fundamentals?

It does. Certainly, the moral norms whose very possibility (as truths) is now disputed are not morality's fundamental principles. Nor do they mark out the whole range of questions of conscience. They are not the whole substance of moral reasonableness, even when this is clarified by the faith which extends beyond belief to action.[1] For, in the relevant sense of "absolute," there are very many moral norms which are true, but not absolute: "Feed your children," for example. This moral norm is true, forceful, but not absolute. When the only food available is the body of your neighbor's living child, one (morally) cannot apply that norm in one's action; nor does one violate it by not applying it.

Still, though relatively few, and though not themselves fundamental, the moral norms whose truth is now contested are decisively important for conscience, conduct, and civilization. And their intrinsic relationship to the foundations of morality and faith is such that to deny them is to overlook, ignore, or challenge those foundations.

---

1. Vatican II, *Lumen Gentium* 25: "the faith which is to be believed and applied to conduct [*fides credenda et moribus applicanda*]."

I shall set up the issue (not settle it) with some words of Pope John Paul II. There is, he says, a "doctrine, based on the Decalogue and on the preaching of the Old Testament, and assimilated into the kerygma of the Apostles and belonging to the earliest teaching of the Church, and constantly reaffirmed by her to this day."[2] "The whole tradition of the Church has lived and lives on the conviction" that "there exist acts which, *per se* and in themselves, independently of circumstances, are always seriously wrong by reason of their object."[3] Correspondingly, "there are moral norms that have a precise content which is immutable and unconditioned . . . for example, the norm . . . which forbids the direct killing of an innocent person."[4] (That is the norm one acknowledges in judging that truly, even if one's own children are starving, one may not kill one's neighbor's sickly child for food.)

These passages speak of actions and their intrinsic wrongness, more than of norms and their absoluteness.[5] And this is fitting. For the absolute moral norms have the following characteristic: The types of action they identify are specifiable, as potential objects of choice, without reliance on any evaluative term which presupposes a moral judgment on the action.[6] Yet this non-

2. Apostolic Exhortation *Reconciliatio et Paenitentia*, 2 December 1984, para. 17 (*Acta Apostolicae Sedis* 77 [1985] 185 at 221).

3. Ibid. See also John Paul II, Address to Moral Theologians, 10 April 1986, para. 3, *Acta Apostolicae Sedis* 78 (1986) 1100: there are human actions which "are always and everywhere in themselves and of themselves illicit."

4. Ibid., para. 4, 1101.

5. See now John Paul II's Address to Moral Theologians of 12 November 1988, para. 5 (*Osservatore Romano* [Eng. ed.] 19–26 December 1988, 7); *Acta Apostolicae Sedis* 81 (1989) 1206–11 at 1209: "By describing the contraceptive act as intrinsically illicit, Paul VI meant to teach that the moral norm is such that it does not admit exceptions. No personal or social circumstances could ever, can now, or will ever, render such an act lawful in itself. The existence of particular norms regarding man's way of acting in the world, which are endowed with a binding force that excludes always and in whatever situation the possibility of exceptions, is a constant teaching of Tradition and of the Church's Magisterium which cannot be called in question by the Catholic theologian."

6. In "Never intentionally kill the innocent," the term *innocent* is doubtless in some sense "evaluative," but the evaluation presupposed (if any) is not an evaluation of the choice and act of killing in those circumstances. Note: In this book, I mean the same by *act* and *action*.

evaluative specification enables moral reflection to judge that the choice of any such act is to be excluded from one's deliberation and one's action.

Thus, the norms in dispute exclude not merely needless acts of city destroying directed against noncombatants and combatants alike, but every act so directed.[7] Not merely those abortions which are chosen as a means to some insufficiently important end, but all killing of unborn babies as a means to an end. Not merely the manufacturing of babies for frivolous or selfish purposes, but all choices to generate babies by production instead of sexual union. Not merely adultery in the sense of extramarital intercourse by (or with) a married person and inadequately attentive to the good of marriage, but adultery as that term was used throughout Jewish and Christian tradition: extramarital intercourse by (or with) a married person, period.

This list of exceptionless norms proposed by Christianity's central moral teachings can easily be continued. But my present aim is to clarify the concept and the terminology. A good label for the disputed absolutes would be *exceptionless moral norms*. For in this context, "absolute" is not to be confused with "absolute" in other contexts, such as the absoluteness of God. The norms in question are not supreme, fundamental, unconditioned; to call them absolute is to say no more than that they are exceptionless.

But they are exceptionless in an interesting way. Exceptions to them are logically possible, and readily conceivable, but are *morally* excluded. In some of them, the type of act is described partly by reference to "circumstances," for example, the circumstance that one of the parties to a sexual act is married to someone else. But of all these norms, the following is true: Once one has precisely formulated the type, one can say that the norm which identifies each chosen act of that type as wrong is true and applicable to every such choice, whatever the (further) circumstances. An exceptionless norm is one which tells us that, when-

7. See the quotation from Vatican II, *Gaudium et Spes* 80, in I.7.

ever we are making a choice, we should never choose to do *that* sort of thing (indeed should never even deliberate about whether or not to do it: see II.1 and IV.3).

Other sorts of norms could be called "exceptionless," but not in an interesting sense of the word. For example: One's completely specific judgments of conscience in particular situations are actually highly specific norms of action,[8] applicable in principle to *such* circumstances on other occasions. And each of these norms is exceptionless, but only by logical, not moral necessity. For such norms, the conscientious judgment that *this is a true norm in all the circumstances* is a judgment which holds good only for *all* such circumstances. Similarly, the disputed moral norms are exceptionless in a way quite different from merely "formal" moral norms which no one will dispute, such as "Do not engage in unjust killing, inordinate sexual intercourse. . . ." Norms of the latter, uncontroversial sort logically cannot have any exceptions, for any morally relevant factors which might suggest an exception have already been implicitly provided for by the norm's own morally evaluative reference ("unjust," "inordinate," and so on) to the very act which the norm concerns.

Moreover, the specific moral absolutes whose *truth* is in dispute do not include "norms" which can artificially be constructed and proposed as exceptionless precisely because the act which they identify is so described that the norm is inapplicable whenever there are morally significant circumstances not mentioned in the norm: for example, "It is always wrong to kill someone *merely* to please another."[9] If, in the circumstances,

---

8. Thus, many who disagree about the absolutes proposed in Christian tradition agree nevertheless that a specific judgment on the rightness of an option "in all the circumstances" is a norm, i.e., a universal in the sense that implicit in the judgment is the rational commitment to judging always in the same way the same option in the same circumstances: e.g., Josef Fuchs, S.J., *Personal Responsibility and Christian Morality* (Washington, D.C.: Georgetown University Press; Dublin: Gill & Macmillan, 1983) 212; Germain Grisez, *The Way of the Lord Jesus*, vol. 1 *Christian Moral Principles* (Chicago: Franciscan Herald Press, 1983) 261, 269.

9. See Fuchs, *Personal Responsibility* 212; Josef Fuchs, *Christian Ethics in a*

pleasing another would have some further good consequences, that norm would not exclude killing an innocent "to please another." Similarly, the norms in dispute are not merely "*practically*" or "*virtually*" exceptionless, like the so-called practical absolutes devised by some theologians as substitutes for the absolutes of Christian tradition. In these substitutes, the act is described by reference to so many and such circumstances that the authors of these norms suppose that, "in practice," further circumstances which might render the act permissible are very unlikely to arise; sometimes they say that exceptions to them are inconceivable, but this is merely a loose use of *conceivable* (to mean likely), or else a confession of limited powers of imagination.[10] But the whole point of the qualifiers *virtually* and *practically* is to signify that if further circumstances were to be added to those referred to in the norm, that norm might no longer be true for this context. The moral absolutes of Christian tradition, on the other hand, are proposed as valid, true, and applicable even in circumstances which are neither foreseen nor even implicitly identified in the norm, but which despite their relevance and moral importance (if they arose) would not deflect the norm's applicability.

Often, the interestingly exceptionless moral norms, the moral absolutes in dispute, are called material, but only, I think, by those who deny their truth. Those who think that some specific,

---

Secular Arena (Washington, D.C.: Georgetown University Press; Dublin: Gill & Macmillan, 1984) 77; Richard A. McCormick, *Notes on Moral Theology 1965 through 1980* (Washington, D.C.: University Press of America, 1981) 710.

10. See, for example, Louis Janssens, "Norms and Priorities in a Love Ethic," *Louvain Studies* 6 (1977) 207 at 217–18; McCormick, *Notes . . . 1965 through 1980* 710–11; Fuchs, *Personal Responsibility* 141, 212, 227–28; Richard M. Gula, *Reason Informed by Faith: Foundations of Catholic Morality* (New York: Paulist Press, 1989) 294; cf. Germain Grisez, *Christian Moral Principles* 165 n. 8; Germain Grisez, "Moral Absolutes: A Critique of the View of Josef Fuchs, S.J.," *Anthropos* [*Anthropotes*] 1985/2, 155 at 181. As McCormick, *Notes . . . 1965 through 1980*, p. 710, says: "One can . . . add a variety of circumstances to the description of an object so that the act is always wrong . . . but when one says that [actions so described are intrinsically wrong], he must realize that he is no longer speaking of the object of the action *as used in recent theological and magisterial literature.*"

exceptionless moral norms are true reject the labels "material," "physical," and "behavioral" (see III.3). So, let me say once for all: save in a few, clearly indicated passages, I shall for brevity use the terms *moral absolutes* or *specific moral absolutes*, meaning absolute and specific moral norms, that is, exceptionless moral norms such as those I mentioned earlier in relation to killing children or noncombatants, adultery, manufacturing babies, and so forth.[11]

2. Witnessed to by faith

The Christian faith affirms specific moral absolutes. Explicitly and implicitly, the New Testament and the Apostolic Fathers, the earliest witnesses to the completed revelation in Christ, resort spontaneously to the Decalogue.[12] Indeed, the Decalogue is referred to more frequently in the New Testament than in the whole of the Old Testament, and the zeal with which Christians preached it (as the one element in the Law still valid in the New Covenant) seems to have provoked its suspension from use in Jewish daily worship and sabbath morning prayers within a few decades after Pentecost.[13] The New Testament and the early

11. Hence, whenever I speak of theologians denying the truth of moral absolutes, I do not imply that those theologians deny the absoluteness and truth of principles which they call formal or transcendental norms.

12. See Guy Bourgeault, "La spécificité de la morale chrétienne selon les Pères des deux premiers siècles, *Science et Esprit* 23 (1971) 137; id. *Décalogue et morale chrétienne: enquête patristique sur l'utilisation et l'interprétation chrétienne du décalogue de c.60 à c.220* (Paris, 1971).

13. See G. Vermes, "The Decalogue and the Minim" [1968], in his *Post-Biblical Jewish Studies* (Leyden: Brill, 1975) 169–77; H. J. Schoeps, *Jewish Christianity* (Philadelphia: Fortress Press, 1969) 34; H. J. Schoeps, *The Jewish-Christian Argument* (New York: Holt, Rhinehart, 1963) 48; W. D. Davies, *The Setting of the Sermon on the Mount* (Cambridge University Press, 1964) 282; F. E. Vokes, "The Ten Commandments in the New Testament and in First Century Judaism," *Studia Evangelica* 5 (1968) 146 at 152; P. Grelot, *Problèmes de morale fondamentale: un éclairage biblique* (Paris: Editions du Cerf, 1982) 117. See also *Encyclopedia Judaica* (Jerusalem: Keter Publishing, 1972), vol. 5 cols. 1446–47. Yet Leo Strauss did not err when he identified "the common ground on which Jews and Christians can make a friendly *collatio* to the secular state" as "the belief in the God of Abraham, Isaac and Jacob—the God who revealed the Ten Commandments or at any rate such commandments as are valid under all circumstances regardless of the circumstances": *Liberalism Ancient and Modern* (New York: Basic Books, 1968) 265–66.

fathers reformulate the Decalogue's prologue and envisage the Ten Commandments as a manifestation of God's sovereignty in the perspective not simply of exodus but now rather of creation itself.[14] St. Paul speaks of its precepts as written on human hearts and befitting human nature (for example, Romans 1:23–31; 2:14–15; by "the Law" in the latter passage he means primarily the Decalogue: see 13:8–10). But these are also precepts of Christ; the Lord is shown reaffirming them in the encounter with the "rich young man" (Matthew 19:16–19; Mark 10:17–19; Luke 18:18–20), interiorizing and in other ways radicalizing (without disincarnating) them in the Sermon on the Mount (Matthew 5:17–28), summarizing without dissolving them in the supreme commandments of love of God and neighbor (Matthew 19:19; 22:36–40), and interpreting them paradigmatically, and with explicit reference to the original order of creation, in his teaching on adultery and the indissolubility of true marriage. "Moses because of the hardness of hearts allowed divorce, but *from the beginning of creation* it was not so; And I [Jesus] say that whoever puts away his wife and marries another commits adultery; and she, if she marries another, commits adultery, too."[15] How is this teaching *paradigmatic*, exemplary? Because in what it plainly asserts, and in its interpretation and transmission in the whole tradition (which the findings of contemporary exegesis have neither challenged nor undermined),[16] it conveys the characteristic or exemplary meaning and force of a specific

14. Bourgeault, "La spécificité," 143–49.
15. Cf. Matt. 19:4–9; Mark 10:4–12; Luke 16:18.
16. The tradition's interpretation of this teaching is not "literalistic" or "fundamentalistic" and is supported by critical exegesis. Still, it is worth recalling here the proper use of exegesis in theology, carefully stated by Vatican II in the last two paragraphs of sec. 12 of the Dogmatic Constitution on Divine Revelation *Dei Verbum*, especially when read with sec. 24; the upshot of these passages is that critical exegesis disengages the possible meanings of the text in one or more hypotheses; it is for the church to pass judgment on which of these possible meanings is indeed what is being asserted in the text. In passing judgment, the church's criteria will be the unity of the Scriptures (so that a possible meaning of *this* can be rejected if it is inconsistent with the meaning of other texts in other books) and the *analogia fidei* in a wider sense (so that a possible meaning which has passed the previous two tests can be rejected if it conflicts with the church's sacred and certain teaching on faith and morals).

moral absolute. It so freshly and specifically identifies differing type-situations (described in nonevaluative terms) in which one commits adultery, that one cannot call it mere *parenesis*—mere exhortation to follow norms whose content is only found elsewhere in the audience's culture, a content neither identified nor reaffirmed by the exhortation. Jesus' teaching includes, then, an element of *instruction*, identifying, clarifying and specifying moral truths, a teaching designed to exclude error and misunderstanding of their proper content.

Thus, we here find adultery understood as always and necessarily wrongful, yet not defined in terms of its wrongfulness. It is not *specified* as wrongful or inordinate or unchaste sex by a married person outside marriage—as sex without proportionate reason. It is defined as sex by a married person outside marriage. The specification needs interpretation and elaboration, since there are questions to be answered about who is indeed married. Christian tradition, as Paul makes clear (1 Corinthians 7), has never treated these questions as simple. But where, as in most cases of adultery, there is no doubt that the one party, if married, is not married to the other, then the Lord's precept applies exceptionlessly, whatever the (other) circumstances.[17]

The same absoluteness of the properly (but still nonevaluatively) specified norm excluding adultery is found in the constant Christian tradition, from the beginning, against abortion,

17. Some say that Paul's directions in 1 Cor. 7:15 treat Jesus' condemnation of divorce as stating a norm of only approximate universality, not truly exceptionless: see Heinz Schürmann, "How Normative Are the Values and Precepts of the New Testament?" in Heinz Schürmann, Ratzinger, and Balthasar, *Principles of Christian Morality* (San Francisco: Ignatius Press, 1986) 26; Heinz Schürmann, "Die Verbindlichkeit konkreter sittlicher Normen nach dem Neuen Testament, bedacht am Beispiel des Ehescheidungsverbotes und im Lichte des Liebesgebotes," in Kerber, ed., *Sittliche Normen: Zum Problem ihrer allgemeinen und unwandelbaren Geltung* (Dusseldorf: Patmos, 1982) 116. But to conclude that Paul regards all Christ's commandments as approximations, whose application is subject to a weighing up and maximizing of greater and lesser premoral expected goods, would be a fallacious inference from the peculiar case of the "Pauline privilege," whose origins in Paul are founded on considerations of another order (the economy of redemption and the identity of sacramental marriage), and which leaves untouched the absoluteness of even the norms against divorce and adultery.

suicide, fornication, homosexual sex, and blasphemy and dis-
claimer of the faith. The tradition is massively solid. It has
cogent grounds, in faith and reason, as we shall see. And it is
witnessed to by martyrdom willingly suffered rather than con-
sent to what the martyr takes to be an act of such a description.
The oppressors, the tempters, the crowd, all persuasively present
the act as an evil lesser than death, disgrace, ruin for the martyr's
family; a Thomas More or a Maria Goretti judges the act to be
wrong *per se* and *in se* and, precisely because immoral, to be an
evil greater than any amount of evil set in train by refusing to
choose such an act.[18] The church judges them to be saints, along
with the many unnamed martyrs.

3. Part of the theology of human fulfillment

The earliest Christian philosophers and systematic theologians
lose little time in developing St. Paul's reflection. As soon as
we meet them, in the second century, they are referring to
the commands of the Decalogue as precepts of natural law, as
the *naturalia legis*, the law's natural precepts, the *naturalia
praecepta quae ab initio infixa dedit hominibus*, the natural
precepts which God from the beginning gave human beings as
intrinsic to their nature, precepts which are natural principles,
befitting the freeborn, and common to all (*naturalia et liberalia
et communia omnium*).[19]

18. See likewise Pius XII, Address to Young Catholic Women, 18 April 1952,
Acta Apostolicae Sedis 44 (1952) 413 at 418, referring to the mother of the
Maccabees and her sons, to Saints Perpetua and Felicity ("despite their new-born
children"), and to St. Maria Goretti. As to More, it is important to note that
when he knowingly incurred the traitor's penalty of life imprisonment and
confiscation of all his goods, for refusing to take an oath, he chose to refuse not
because the oath was against the faith (e.g., against the doctrine of the papacy),
but because swearing that he believed a marriage invalid when he judged it valid
would have been to lie. He went to the Tower on a simple point of morality, the
absoluteness of the ordinary norm which excludes lying, most clearly lying on
oath.

19. St. Irenaeus, *Adversus Haereses* (circa 180–199) 4, 13,1; 15,1; 16,5; see
also St. Theophilus of Antioch, *To Autolycus* (circa 181) 2, 16–17 (PG 6, 1079):
to observe the law of God is to live according to nature [*kata physin*].

This means not merely that they are rational norms, available (as Justin stresses)[20] to the non-Christian conscience which is not blinded by depravity. It means also that they guide one toward human fulfillment, by disclosing the plan, the mind, the *consilium* of God for that fulfillment. As Irenaeus puts it, God has no need of our love; it is we who have need of God's glory, which can in no way be attained save through service of God; and to prepare us for this life of friendship with God and concord with neighbor, the Lord articulated the Decalogue, which Jesus reaffirmed, amplified, and perfected.[21]

The link between the Decalogue and human fulfillment is no mere construction of early theologians. It is intrinsic.

For human fulfillment is the fulfillment of persons, in community; above all it is constituted by participation in the perfected community of the Kingdom which Christ will hand over to the Father. Each of the precepts of the second table of the Decalogue protects some aspect of human persons in some fundamental aspect of their individual reality. Thus, given the Christian conception of the significance of free choice (see III.1), each of those precepts, and each of the specific moral absolutes proposed to us by the tradition,[22] is to be understood as an implication of the supreme principles: "Love God above all things," "Love your neighbor as yourself," and "Seek first the Kingdom." The precepts protecting fundamental aspects of human personal good

20. St. Justin the Martyr, *Dialogue with Trypho* (circa 155) c.93,1: God shows every race of man what is always and under all conditions [*semper et modis omnibus*] right . . . and people of every sort know that adultery, fornication, murder, etc., are wrong.

21. Irenaeus thus links the Decalogue to his theology of human fulfillment: "the glory of God is living man, but the life of man is the vision of God" [*gloria enim Dei vivens homo, vita autem hominibus visio Dei*]: *Adversus Haereses* IV, 20,7; see also IV, 4,2; 8,2; 12,5; 13,1 and 3; 16,3 and 4; 18,3; 34,4.

22. In traditional theology and catechesis, each absolute was often considered to be implicit in a precept of the Decalogue. E.g., "Do not commit adultery" can be understood not as merely a formal paranetic call for responsible sexual conduct but as the paradigmatic expression of a series of specific moral absolutes excluding not only adultery *stricto sensu* but also fornication, homosexual sex, and other (singly or mutually) masturbatory activities. But there is no theological necessity to regard, say, all the absolutes concerning sex as implicit in "Do not commit adultery": see, e.g., Aquinas, *Summa Theologiae* 1–2 q.100 a.11.

are guides to human choice; they guide by excluding options inconsistent with love of the very person whom the logic of our choosing makes our nearest neighbor.[23]

In the Synoptics and Paul; in Irenaeus, Augustine, Aquinas, and Vatican II, and in common Christian faith, teaching, and belief, right action is not blind submission to unintelligible will. Rather, right action is the wisdom of action which expresses a heart really in line with, toward, the ultimate human end and good, the integral human fulfillment which cannot be found outside that Kingdom whose material is being formed here on earth but whose completion lies beyond history.[24] The rightness of action is always intelligibly related to human good, indeed to the good of particular individuals or groups of individual persons. The upright heart, the will, the choice, is always a choice, will, heart which does and pursues that good and avoids what harms that good.

There is never a case in which to adhere to a true specific moral absolute is thereby to "honor rules above values."[25] Rather, in adhering to the moral truth articulated by the "rule," one honors the value, the person whose good in some fundamental respect one would be choosing to destroy, damage, or impede, by the act which the norm specifies as always to be excluded from deliberation, choice, and action. (The person so honored may be oneself, as when one rejects suicide or other self-destructive or self-disintegrating actions.) And one does not thereby dishonor, discount, or in any way reject the values, the human goods which one supposes could be secured by violating the moral absolute. Indeed, in deliberating and arriving at one's moral judgment, one does not even rank them as lesser in value

23. Cf. John Paul II, Encyclical *Sollicitudo Rei Socialis*, 30 December 1987, para. 36: "the 'second tablet' of the Ten Commandments (cf. Exod. 20:12–17; Deut. 5:16–21). Not to observe these is to offend God and hurt one's neighbour, and to introduce into the world influences and obstacles which go far beyond the actions and brief lifespan of an individual."

24. *Gaudium et Spes* 38 (*terreno . . . servitio . . . materiam regni caelestis parantes*) 39.

25. As is alleged by Garth Hallett, *Christian Moral Reasoning* (Notre Dame, Ind., and London: Notre Dame University Press, 1983) 120.

than the human good respected by adherence to the moral absolute. Here, prior to moral judgment and choice, greater and lesser amounts of goodness are not the issue. They *cannot* be the issue (II.5).

There are hard cases, as everybody knows. The prospect of loss of human good (of persons), of damage apparently avertable by violating the moral absolute, can seem indubitable and be felt as overwhelming. But these are cases in which we do not see the relevant parts of the scheme of providence—a scheme of which we never, in this life, see the whole or even much. (I say this to recall a relevant aspect of the human situation, not as an argument *for* the truth of moral absolutes.) In these cases, then, the moral absolutes call for a refusal to dishonor the basic human good directly at stake in our choice; they call us to leave providence to settle the "balance" of human goods, a balance which we would merely deceive ourselves if we supposed we could truly see and settle for ourselves.

Right human action's ultimate rational criterion is its relationship to human persons precisely in their fullest good. And that fullest human good in fact consists in the participation of persons in the Kingdom of God, present now but only "in mystery" (*Gaudium et Spes* 39) and "under construction." Thus, no one in the Christian tradition supposed that the rightness of action consisted in its efficacy, its effectiveness, real or envisaged, in bringing about the ultimate human end and good. Each of us must exist and work on some fragmentary part of the building up of the Kingdom. Its completion is in the hands of divine providence and grace. To hope to take on the architectonic role of providence is not wisdom but folly.

4. Rejected when human replaces divine providence

However insecurely the specific moral absolutes are articulated and affirmed outside Christian faith, the formal rejection of all such absolutes, the claim that none of them can be true, is a post-Christian phenomenon.

It emerges in the eighteenth and nineteenth centuries among such men as Bentham and Marx. They rejected Christianity, rebelled against the false moral-cultural absolutes unjustly protecting property and status, and in their hopes and intentions transposed the Christian conception of a Kingdom—of a Kingdom built up by faith and good works brought to transcendent fruition by divine grace and providence. By this transposition of hope, the Kingdom was transformed into the inner-worldly realm of justice, prosperity, fraternity, and freedom, to be constructed by enlightened human planning and providence.

Today, Benthamite and Marxian ambitions to take charge of history are generally felt to be empty presumption. But their modeling of ethical deliberation and judgment on technical assessment and judgment—a modeling which the whole pre-Enlightenment ethical tradition had envisaged only to reject—remains powerfully attractive. Technical thinking, after all, is ubiquitous and yields many desirable and/or desired consequences. It is, moreover, the thought-form of children, as soon as they become able to organize themselves to get what they want. One envisages a determinate goal which can be attained by thoughtful disposition of effective means; scrutinizes alternative courses of action for their efficacy as means and their cost in terms of other goals; and selects and undertakes the action promising to be most effective in attaining the goal with least cost.

Catholics who formally deny the truth of the tradition's specific absolutes do not envisage an ultimate human goal or end comparable to Bentham's or Marx's. (I leave to one side some "liberation theologians.")[26] They reject utilitarianism's impoverished conception of human good, and Marx's fantasy of the all-round man liberated from the division of labor and from the

26. But it is important not to lose sight of the attack on moral absolutes from theologians embedded not in a North Atlantic culture desirous of sexual liberties, abortion, nuclear deterrence, and euthanasia, but in a third world context desirous of pragmatically efficacious means of advancing revolutionary liberation; e.g., Juan Luis Segundo, *Liberation of Theology* (Maryknoll, N.Y.: Orbis Books, 1976) 154–75.

disposition to raise questions about the ultimate source of existence, meaning and value. Some of them accept a sound theory of the basic goods:[27] goods in recognizing which one recognizes the basic forms of human flourishing and thus the potentialities of human nature. But virtually none of them does serious work in basic moral theory. Their theories, although far more ambitious than the few modest theses of 1963/64 (see IV.1–3), are each intended by most (though not all) of them as a principle for resolving what they call "conflict" or "borderline" situations, rather than as a general ethical method. They take for granted as much of the tradition as they find helpful; they lack understanding of its organic philosophical and theological unity and propose alterations without having an overall plan of renewal, or a clear conception of where the foundations lie. (So, whatever their good intentions, their work brings the whole structure tumbling down, in the minds of those who value that work.)

Though limited in intended scope, the principle and method of these theologians shares in the Enlightenment conception of morality: One's ultimate and immediate responsibility is to bring about good states of affairs in the world and (here they wrongly suppose that this is the same or a consistent, not a competing principle)[28] to prevent the occurrence of bad states of affairs. And if *some* good, then, of course, *more* good. Hence their characteristic moral principle and method: Pursue the course which promises, in itself and its consequences, a net greater proportion of good states of affairs, or (again, too casually supposed to be a coapplicable criterion) a net lesser proportion of bad, overall, in the long run. For the sake of a label, let us call this "proportionalism."[29] Often proportionalists will add that

27. See, e.g., Richard McCormick, S.J., *How Brave a New World?* (London: SCM Press, 1981) 5.

28. See John Finnis, *Fundamentals of Ethics* (Washington, D.C.: Georgetown University Press, 1983) 88–89.

29. The label is for brevity. It is not a term of abuse or a substitute for definition and argument. It is a label which many proponents of such a principle are happy to apply to their principle and method, e.g., Josef Fuchs, *Christian Morality: The Word Becomes Flesh* (Washington, D.C.: Georgetown University

this responsibility, self-evidently, *is* the requirement of love of God and neighbor which Jesus came to teach and exemplify.[30]

Why did no one in the Catholic tradition until about twenty years ago, and no one in the Protestant tradition until about fifty years ago,[31] articulate this "self-evident" principle (save, in effect, to reject it)? The philosophical answer I shall develop in chapter III. The theological answer is one which (see III.2) Paul already indicated in Romans 3 and 6. But here I shall give it in an independent form, as a reductio ad absurdum.

Divine providence involves the permission of evil (of any and every kind) only so that out of it God may draw a somehow greater good.[32] So, if the supreme or decisive moral responsibility is to pursue a state of affairs embodying greater good, the moral norm in every problem-situation would be, quite simply, Try anything. That is, Do whatever you feel like! For if you accomplish what you attempt, you can be certain that what you chose tended toward overall long-run net good (since God's

---

Press; Dublin: Gill & Macmillan, 1987) 16; Edward V. Vacek, S.J., "Proportionalism: One View of the Debate" *Theological Studies* 46 (1985) 287. On the relationships among the labels *proportionalist, teleological, consequentialist* (and *utilitarian*), see Finnis, *Fundamentals of Ethics* 80–86. There are, of course, differences among proportionalists about the meaning, content, and application of their method; the struggles of Richard McCormick, S.J., to articulate a viable version have resulted in a particularly instructive mélange. As I explain at a number of points later, the common theme is more important than the variations; the criticisms I shall address to the former are of general applicability.

30. Even more boldly, Garth Hallett, *Christian Moral Reasoning* 82, 121, 189, 193, claims that the single criterion of moral judgment is "Maximize value, minimize disvalue," and that this is the relevant moral meaning of Christ's "Have life and have it more abundantly" (John 5:40)!

31. Emil Brunner, *The Divine Imperative* ([1932] London, 1937) 196–97, 613, has perhaps a certain priority here. But it is clear that by the beginning of the twentieth century, Protestant theologians had generally given up any basis of principle on which to resist the advance of secular arguments that there are no means which cannot be justified by some good end: see Joseph Mausbach, *Catholic Moral Teaching and Its Antagonists* ([1900] New York, 1914) 86–89.

32. Aquinas, *Commentum in librum II sententiarum* d.29, q.1, a.3, ad 4: "Deus ex malo semper maius bonum elicit [quam illud bonum quod per malum privatur], non tamen illi de necessitate in quo malum esse permittit, sed in comparatione ad universum, cuius pulchritudo consistit ex hoc quod mala esse sinuntur." See Guy de Broglie S.J., "Malice intrinsèque du péché et péchés heureux par leurs conséquences," *Recherches de Science Religieuse* 24 (1934) 302 at 306–8.

providence permitted it), whereas if you fail to accomplish what you attempt, you can be certain that your failure tended toward overall long-run net good since God's providence excluded the success of your effort. So, try anything!

But it is patently absurd to accept the maxim, If in doubt try anything.[33] Thus the proportionalist moral method, whether advanced as the method of ethics or only as a principle for resolving conflict situations, is inconsistent with a Christian understanding of divine providence. (Indeed, it confuses human with divine providence, and human responsibility with God's.)[34]

5. No narrowing of horizons

A principal proportionalist objection to the truth of specific moral absolutes is this: They irrationally abstract *some* elements from the total reality of a human action. Reason, objectivity, and truth require that an action be evaluated only as a totality—a totality which includes all the circumstances and motivations, considered in relation to all the premoral (but morally relevant) goods and bads involved in that totality—with a view to ascertaining the behavior which will effect overall net human good. But in adhering to a moral absolute one rejects an option as soon as one understands it as including an action of the type specified in the norm, and thus one narrows one's focus unreasonably (see also IV.3).

Now, this objection is certainly unsound. To judge one's option *right*, one must consider all morally relevant circum-

---

33. Is it necessary to add that nothing in the foregoing argument suggests that proportionalists intend to teach "Try anything" or "Do what you feel like"? The point of the argument is to show that these morally absurd injunctions are entailed by what the proportionalists do teach, taken together with a theological doctrine which they do or should accept.

34. This confusion is sometimes explicit, as in Hallett, *Christian Moral Reasoning* 120: "If Christian charity should resemble the divine, then the knowledge and values which guide Providence should guide our actions too, with like results, so far as we can attain to that ideal." Hallett thus contends that the true ethical criterion, "maximization of value," is to be adopted because it is "the ethics of God himself" (id.). At the same time, he admits that the consequences of actions are endlessly varied and "known to God alone" (id.)

stances—*bonum ex integra causa*. But one can judge an agent's action *wrong* as soon as one identifies a morally significant defect in one's motivations, or an inappropriateness in relation either to the circumstances or to the means involved in that option—*malum ex quocumque defectu*.[35] In other words, one who, in accordance with a moral absolute, excludes an option as wrong is not excused from doing everything morally possible to pursue the goods which could have been sought by violating the moral absolute. Such a person's horizons are in no way narrowed.[36] Indeed, the situation thus morally structured challenges the chooser to expand the horizons of possibility with creativity and zeal. Whereas bureaucrats encourage the poor to solve their problems by contralife choices, those who exclude such practices from their deliberations, out of respect for life, have often expanded the bounds of medical care and treatment, and of the nurture of children.

The irony, then, is this: Those who undertake to assess and compare the amounts of premoral but humanly relevant goods and bads promised in alternative options are *bound* to narrow their focus, to shrink the horizons of their assessment. (For only thus can they make the assessment and comparison even *seem* possible.)[37] And this narrowing cannot be guided by any *moral*

35. The specific source of the scholastic tag is "Dionysius," *De divinis nominibus* (circa 500) 4, 22 (*PG* 3, 729): "quilibet singularis defectus causat malum, bonum autem causatur ex integra causa"; the thought, as expounded previously, is of primary importance in St. Thomas' explanation of morality in *Summa Theol.* 1–2 qq.18–20; see initially, q.18 a.4 ad 3; also 9.19 a.6 ad 1; q.71 a.5 ad 1; 2–2 q. 79 a.3 ad 4; *De malo* q.2 a.1 ad 3, a.4 ad 2; *In eth. II* lect. 7 (n. 320).

36. The claim that those who conscientiously refuse to violate moral absolutes for the sake of "greater good" thereby manifest a lesser or narrower willingness to further human good is made by Bruno Schüller, S.J., "The Double Effect in Catholic Thought: A Reevaluation," in Richard McCormick, S.J., and Paul Ramsey, *Doing Evil to Achieve Good* (Chicago: Loyola University Press, 1978) 191; see also Richard McCormick, S.J., *Doing Evil* 241, 243. The fallaciousness of this claim is explored in John Finnis, "The Act of the Person" in *Persona, Verità e Morale*, Atti del Congresso Internazionale de Teologia Morale (Rome: Città Nuova Editrice, 1987) 159 at 169–73.

37. See, e.g., Hallett, *Christian Moral Reasoning* 159: "obviously the perfection of the whole [e.g, of a Rembrandt picture] is something more than the sum of its parts' perfections. And might not the same be said of our actions, indeed of our lives, as wholes. . . ? Must not a contemplated divorce, for instance, be seen in its

principle of responsibility. For *either*, Pursue the greater pre-moral good is their exclusive moral principle,[38] *or* at least they maintain that moral principles generally applicable are *overridden* by the proportion of premoral goods and bads promised by one option compared with others in a situation of "conflict." Hence, in their inescapable narrowing of horizons, proportionalists are, willy-nilly, guided primarily by what they happen to want, by desire, not reason.

For: The task of commensurating the goods and bads involved in alternative options—where this commensurating is proposed as governing, not governed by, moral principles and norms of responsibility—is well beyond human reason's power to encompass. The goods and bads involved, for example, in bringing a child into the world go far beyond those which a couple can envisage as they try to compare not having a child with having one and bringing it up over the next twenty years. Again, the goods and bads involved in nuclear destruction of Hiroshima and Nagasaki extend to include far more than the numbers of lives destroyed or damaged then and there compared with the number of lives at stake in a seaborne invasion of Japan.

Thus, a couple who settle the morality of a contralife choice (precisely to impede the coming-to-be of a possible baby) by

---

relation to the institution of marriage. . . ? A negative answer is as impossible as an affirmative. [!] For we . . . do not enjoy the sort of overall view for which [a list of merits and demerits of this divorce] would be a precondition, and thus cannot take the further step of comparing the synthetic whole with the analytic summation. Analytic, piecemeal evaluation [Hallett's ethical method] is justified . . . by the fact that [an intuitive grasp of the whole], of a whole society or institution, is forever beyond us . . . a great many economic, social, political, and ecclesial decisions demand consideration of so vast a tableau that the human mind can only peruse it flashlightwise, sector by sector."

38. Some, like Hallett, *Christian Moral Reasoning* 164–65, while proposing the single principle or "criterion," viz., "maximize value," are willing to include in the "calculation" not only premoral but also "moral benefits and harms," e.g., "sin," as "values" or "disvalues" which can be outweighed by other values. Hallett's solution to the manifest problems of commensurability is simple: (i) the "calculation" is by intuition rather than reason (p. 160) and (ii) moral and premoral values (disvalues) have this in common: they are all values (disvalues); therefore [!] they can be commensurated; see also his "The 'Incommensurability' of Values," *Heythrop Journal* 28 (1987) 373 at 376.

telling themselves that they are choosing a lesser amount of premoral evil have, willy-nilly, narrowed the horizons of their assessment. What makes them feel that the future without the baby will be better than the future with it is their not wanting the possible baby and certain of the likely consequences of the baby's coming to be. To know—that is, to make a *rational* judgment—that the one future embodies more premoral good than any and all of its alternatives would be to know and understand the future, both of this world and of the Kingdom, in a manner that lies utterly outside the reach of human providence. (Of course, one can make a moral judgment that we should not have another baby, and one can express that moral judgment by saying that not having another baby is, in the situation, the greater good. But this moral judgment is not made by aggregating premoral goods and bads so as to identify the sort of "greater good" or "lesser evil" which proportionalists need in order to *arrive* at moral judgment. Often, it will be a judgment guided by, and relative to, the particular commitments which the couple have made, commitments not required by reason but adopted by a vocational choice responsive to feelings entirely personal to that couple. In any event, it will be a moral judgment which takes its place alongside, not above, other moral norms.)

Or again: The attempt to settle the morality of intentionally killing noncombatants in Hiroshima and Nagasaki (not to mention Hamburg and Dresden), by assessing amounts of premoral good at stake, was bound to involve, and did involve, a drastic shrinking of horizons. It was so drastic and arbitrary that even the amoral historian readily notices how the decision-procedure overlooked or arbitrarily discounted relevant alternatives (such as maintaining an air and sea blockade together with discriminating attacks on Japan's dwindling residue of naval, air, and military forces or, more fundamentally, renouncing the declared goal of unconditional surrender to which all strategic, political, and moral thinking had been subordinated as if to a simple, *given* technical objective). The consequences, bad and good, of deciding to force unconditional surrender by staging a gigantic massacre of civilians are not even remotely exhausted yet and remain overall far beyond assessment by human *reason.*

In short: To deny the truth of moral absolutes by arguing that they block the reasonable and responsible pursuit of greater amounts of premoral human good is incoherent with faith in divine providence. It results, necessarily, in reducing morality to a pseudotechnical reasoning in pursuit of goals defined not by reason (or morality) but by feelings which shrink the horizon of deliberation in order to create the illusion of commensurating what is in reality rationally incommensurable. By contrast, to respect the moral absolutes which are made known to us by God through reason and faith is to cooperate with God, who has practical knowledge of everything without limit. And to cooperate thus with God is to *take into account everything* (the principal demand of proportionalists), *in the only way we can.*

6. Choice, reflexivity, and proportionalism

But there is a further range of reasons why the tradition, both of philosophy and of faith, treated as obviously untenable what proportionalists today profess to be self-evident. These reasons concern the reflexivity of moral choice, the "intransitive"[39] significance of freely chosen action.

Secular philosophical discussions of proportionalism have been more penetrating and careful than the publications of theologians denying the truth of absolutes. Some secular philosophers have noted that if one tries to settle problems of choice by predicting anticipated proportions of premoral goods and bads, one becomes a different sort of person; one stands ready to do and become anything, for the sake of becoming a mere conduit

---

39. Cf. Karol Wojtyla, *The Acting Person* (Dordrecht, Boston, London: Reidel, 1979) 13, 98–99, 109, 150–51, 161, on the "intransitivity" of action; in his encyclical *Laborem Exercens*, 14 September 1981, para. 6 this is referred to as the "subjective aspect" of work, as distinct from work's "objective" or "transitive" aspect (its effect on objects).

through which history will work greater amounts of good or lesser amounts of bad.[40] Some such philosophers have, indeed, felt obliged to concede that this reflexive consequence of adopting proportionalism might make adopting it the greater evil: Adhering to the moral absolutes would yield better outcomes, not because of the obvious risk of miscalculation of outcomes and their respective value(s), but because this reflexive outcome is so significant and undesirable.[41]

But we should neither seek nor accept this concession. We should be content with the more accurate reflection: This sort of consequence simply cannot be commensurated with the other features and consequences of one's particular choices. Whether good or bad, the sacrifice it requires, of personal commitments and stable identity, involves goods or harms of a type radically different from the lives lost, prevented, preserved, or initiated, from the truths concealed or disclosed; and so on. And the effect of choices on one's identity and character is radically different from the effects of any of the other bringings about, blockings, or damagings of instantiations of human goods by chosen activity.[42]

Consider another example of reflexivity, the reflexivity of a decision less abstract than the decision to adopt proportionalism and deny the truth of any specific moral absolutes. Maintaining a nuclear deterrent for the sake of liberty and justice and the rule of law has morally significant implications going far beyond its effectiveness in maintaining those goods of social life. These implications include also the impact on the human well-being, and on the whole moral life, of those who make or are willing to carry out the threat to carry out a final retaliatory massacre and

---

40. See, e.g., J. J. C. Smart and Bernard Williams, *Utilitarianism For and Against* (Cambridge University Press, 1973) 116–18; Bernard Williams, *Moral Luck* (Cambridge University Press, 1981) 41–53; Samuel Scheffler, *The Rejection of Consequentialism* (Oxford University Press, 1982) chaps. 1 and 2.

41. See, e.g., Derek Parfit, *Reasons and Persons* (Oxford University Press, 1984) 24–28, 43.

42. For another consideration of the ways in which reflexivity blocks proportionalist reasoning, see Bartholomew M. Kiely, S.J., "The Impracticability of Proportionalism," *Gregorianum* 66 (1985) 655–86.

demolition of an enemy society. Equally, if the deterrent were unilaterally renounced out of reverence for human life, the morally significant implications of that renunciation would go far beyond its effectiveness in preventing death. These implications would include also the impact on human well-being, and on the whole moral life, of a willingness to undergo tyrannous domination rather than be ready to carry out vast massacres. And the implications, which I do not prejudge, would differ widely according to the reasons for this willingness. If the reason were of the form Better Red than dead, the implications would be very different from those of a willingness to accept anything, even martyrdom, rather than do wrong. The one thing clear is that human reason cannot possibly make a comparative assessment of all these implications, all these different types and possible instantiations of goods and bads, so as to arrive at a conclusion of the form, Reason, guiding rather than guided by moral judgments, identifies one of these options as promising overall greater net good, or net lesser evil, than its alternatives.

The reflexive significance of action was pointed to by Aristotle, when he observed that making (poiesis) differs from doing (praxis), that is, technology from morality, and that the decisive point of human praxis is the activity itself.[43] Thus Aristotle indicated that chosen actions make an important difference not only to the matters which agents are trying to achieve or avoid but also, willy-nilly, to the agents themselves (and in another way, to anyone who admires them or adopts their principles of action).

Christian reflection, taking its cue from the Old Testament (Deuteronomy 30:19, Sirach 15:11–20), identified the ground of the morally significant reflexivity of actions: free choice.[44] Since a choice is free precisely inasmuch as it is settled by nothing

---

43. See *Nicomachean Ethics* 6,4: 1140b3–6; John M. Cooper, *Reason and Human Good in Aristotle* (Cambridge, Mass.: Harvard University Press, 1975) 2, 78, 111.

44. For the Christian sources, see Grisez, *Christian Moral Principles* 41–44, 61–62.

whatever except the chooser's own act of choosing, it has a truly originating, creative, soul-making significance. It is no accident that the pioneers of proportionalist moral methodology, Bentham and Mill, denied the reality of free choice.[45] Rejecting that reality, they could believe that moral deliberation and judgment are a quasi-technical matter of finding one's way to the greater good, or the less bad state of affairs. For, denying free choice, they could ignore the soul-making significance of moral action.

Equally, it is no accident that among the moral theologians who have adopted the methodology, several (perhaps many)[46] leave little or no room, in depicting human personal reality, for the free choices whose constitutive significance Christian dogma, practice, and theology so emphasized.

Later I shall make a different (not unrelated) point about free choice (II.4): The proportionalist belief in the commensurability of the premoral goods involved in alternative possibilities is incompatible with belief that there is any rationally motivated free choice which an identification of the greater net premoral good (or lesser evil) might guide aright. But the incommensurability of reflexive with nonreflexive goods and bads already

45. See Jeremy Bentham, *An Introduction to the Principles of Morals and Legislation*, ed. J. H. Burns and H. L. A. Hart, (1789; reprint London and New York: Methuen, 1982) 11 (chap. 1, para. 1), 134 (chap. 11, para. 28); John Stuart Mill, *A System of Logic* (1843) bk. 6, chaps. 2 and 11; *An Examination of Sir William Hamilton's Philosophy* (1865) chap. 26. Of course, *free choice* is not an unequivocal term, and Mill, like many others ("compatibilists," "soft determinists"), accepts a distinction between choices which are free or voluntary in the sense of uncoerced though not uncaused and choices which are unfree because coerced. On theological rather than Enlightenment philosophical grounds, Michel du Bay, *De libero hominis arbitrio eiusque potestate* (Louvain, 1563), c.7, formulates the soft determinist position quite neatly: "What comes about voluntarily comes about freely even if it comes about necessarily." (This proposition was condemned by Pope Pius V in 1567: *Denz-Schoen* 1939.) See also Aquinas's formulation (and rejection as heretically subversive of all moral thought) of a similar soft determinist position, *De malo* q.6 a. un. resp. On the whole matter of free choice, see Joseph Boyle, Germain Grisez, and Olaf Tollefsen, *Free Choice: A Self-Referential Argument* (Notre Dame, Ind.: Notre Dame University Press, 1976).

46. See, e.g., T. E. O'Connell, *Principles for a Catholic Morality* (New York: Seabury Press, 1978) 59, 62; cf. Finnis, "Act of the Person," 160–168.

gives us sufficient reason to conclude that reason does not and cannot show that a specific moral absolute, protecting a basic aspect of human personal reality against any and every choice to destroy, damage, or impede it, is unreasonable. Reasoning which appeals to the balance of premoral goods and bads is impotent to show that any of the moral absolutes transmitted to us by the tradition is untrue.

7. Protecting changeless aspects of human fulfillment

But not all denials of the truth of exceptionless moral norms are predicated on such an appeal. Some are based on the view that no moral norm, or no moral norm with the specificity of the tradition's absolutes, could possibly be exceptionless; for none can be permanent, but all must be subject to change, because human nature, at least in the relevant respects, is changeable.

In the nearly two decades since Karl Rahner give this thesis voice and vogue,[47] it has been widely repeated and adopted. But it remains as sketchily explained and lightly defended as at its launching. Rahner himself never ventured to make clear what he thought changeable and what constant in human nature, or how he thought any moral norm is "based on" human nature; he merely talked abstractly about concrete as opposed to trans-cendent human nature. A sound moral theory does not deduce moral norms from some presupposed knowledge of human nature, but rather from an understanding of the basic aspects of human fulfillment.[48] Neither Rahner nor anyone else has

47. Karl Rahner, S.J., "Basic Observations on the Subject of Changeable and Unchangeable Factors in the Church" [1970], in his *Theological Investigations* 14 (New York: Crossroad, 1976) 15: "nowadays indeed . . . the immediate norm of natural morality is subject [to swift changes], the norm being man himself in his *concrete nature.*" For further references and critique, see John Finnis, "The Natural Law, Objective Morality, and Vatican II" in William E. May, *Principles of Catholic Moral Life* (Chicago: Franciscan Herald Press, 1980) 113 at 139–42, 148–49; Grisez, *Christian Moral Principles* 869 n. 62.

48. See John Finnis, "Natural Inclinations and Natural Rights: Deriving 'Ought' from 'Is' According to Aquinas," in J. Elders and K. Hedwig, *Lex et Libertas: Freedom and Law According to St. Thomas Aquinas*, Studi Tomistici, no. 30 (Rome: Libreria Editrice Vaticana, 1987) 43–49.

made any serious or even noticeable effort to indicate a change in any of the basic aspects of human fulfillment, that is, in the goods which are protected by the tradition's specific moral absolutes.

The position, then, remains exactly as stated by Vatican II in *Gaudium et Spes (GS)*. There, having indicated the modern world's dynamic of change, the council affirmed:

> The Church also maintains that beneath all changes there are many realities which do not change and which have their ultimate foundation in Christ, who is the same yesterday and today, yes and forever. Hence in the light of Christ, the image of the unseen God, the first-born of every creature, the Council wishes to speak to all men in order to illuminate the mystery of man and to cooperate in solving the principal questions of our time. (*GS* 10)

Approaching then the question of war, "the Council wishes to recall first of all the permanent binding force of the natural law of peoples and its universal principles" (*GS* 79). Immediately the council goes on to denounce "actions deliberately opposed" to these permanent principles, actions which are not excused by being done simply in obedience to superior orders (*GS* 79). (This dismissive reference to the obedience-to-orders motive eliminates any possibility that the "principles" the council has in mind are merely formal principles defining acts in terms of immoral motives.) The council then solemnly pronounces a specific moral absolute: "Every act of war which is directed indiscriminately to the destruction of whole towns or wide areas with their inhabitants is a crime against God and man" (*GS* 80).[49] No one has yet tried to indicate how a change in human nature might render untrue a moral norm which was pronounced in reflective judgment on acts most of which had, only twenty years earlier, been carried out in the just cause of defending human civilization and indeed the church against the genocidal Nazi enemy.

To be sure, historicity and social change do affect moral

49. As the political and religious terminology of the period makes clear, *indiscriminately* here is not a moral or other evaluative qualifier, like *disproportionately*, but signifies an intention to kill noncombatants along with combatants.

judgment. Social and cultural entities such as borrowing and lending change; the development of a capital market linking interest on loans with the return on joint productive enterprises means that outwardly similar behavior, in 1288 and in 1988, can involve very different relationships between the wills of those doing it and the relevant human goods: same behavior, different actions (see II.2). Again, options can be transformed by conceptual clarification. A correct moral judgment on the position which mingled religious freedom with indifferentism[50] can be transformed, for example, into two correct moral judgments on alternatives now adequately differentiated. Again, emotional biases which blocked differentiation, for example between penal servitude and chattel *servitudo*, can be removed by changed social conditions, allowing the latent moral insight to be clearly articulated, as in the specific moral absolute which excludes slavery. Or new or apparently new forms of behavior, such as taking the pill, can raise the question whether they are instances of a familiar and more or less well understood form of action, such as contraception, and that question can clarify and deepen understanding of that action and of precisely why one does wrong in willing it. Finally, other new behavior may prove, on analysis, to be indeed a new form of action, such as baby production, a new form of action, but one which turns out to possess one morally decisive feature in common with the fairly recently clarified moral evil of slavery.[51]

50. Or with the opinion that religious liberty entails that religious vows are neither morally binding nor even morally proper (e.g., the decision of the French revolutionary Constituent Assembly of 12/13 February 1790); or with the opinion that liberty of forming and publicly expressing opinion must be absolutely untrammeled (e.g., the teachings of Lamennais's liberal Catholic newspaper *L'Avenir* beginning in 1830 and condemned by Pope Gregory XVI's *Mirari Vos* in 1832: see Brian Harrison, *Religious Liberty and Contraception* [Melbourne: John XXIII Fellowship Co-operative, 1988] 34–42).

51. See *Donum Vitae* (Congregation for the Doctrine of the Faith, Instruction on Respect for Human Life in Its Origin and on the Dignity of Procreation, 22 February 1987) 2.B.4–5 (*Acta Apostolicae Sedis* 80 [1988] 70 at 91–94); John C. Ford, Germain Grisez, Joseph Boyle, John Finnis and William E. May, *The Teaching of Humanae Vitae: A Defense* (San Francisco: Ignatius Press, 1988) 95–97.

All such historical changes and developments are remote indeed from the talked-of but never specified "changes in human nature." Indeed, they are very remote from something pervasive in publications denying the truth of exceptionless moral norms—the pervasive and unhistorical sense of remoteness from, and moral superiority to, the past from which those moral absolutes have been transmitted to us. A representative passage from a theological publication of the type:

> That [yesteryear] was the age in which man was convinced he knew right from wrong. . . . Doubt as to the rectitude of one's conduct was easily dispelled. A glance at any of the standard moral texts made it so easy to judge the moral quality of any given human action. . . . Surety was easy to be had in a world not yet sensitive to the full range of human values. Certainty was relatively easy to attain when a small number of decisions had to be made. . . . Virtual unanimity was easy to come by when all men and women faced almost identical sets of circumstances in their lives.[52]

As a portrayal of Socrates' Athens, of the Roman empire of Jesus and Paul, the Lyon of Irenaeus, the collapsing imperium of Augustine of Hippo, or the new city culture of Bonaventure and Thomas Aquinas, such a word picture is indeed a burlesque. On abortion, infanticide, suicide, adultery, contraception, homosexual sex, theft, and lying, moral norms were addressed to the consciences of the men and women of those days in circumstances *no less complex and varied* than today's.

Nor was it ever the case that a glance at a standard moral text made it easy to judge the moral quality of any given action. Everything in the New Testament, Augustine, and Thomas (and much in Plato and Aristotle) tells you that judging the rightness of action is no easy task but is the task of virtue, of discerning one's vocation and following it out with creativity, intelligence, fairness, humility, and all the other needful dispositions. The moral absolutes now in dispute identify wrong actions, not right; they are negative norms (*praecepta negativa*) which hold

---

52. Raymond F. Collins, "Foreword," *Louvain Studies* 6 (1977) 206.

good always and on every occasion (*semper et ad semper*), whereas the many other essential and affirmative moral principles and norms (*praecepta affirmativa*) hold good *semper sed non ad semper*—are always somehow relevant but leave it to your moral judgment to discern the times, places, and other circumstances of their directiveness.[53]

8. Negative norms but positive and revelatory

The dialectic of negative and positive in the moral life is even richer than I have just suggested. This is made clear in Germain Grisez's discussion of the moral absolute on adultery:

The meaning of the good of marital love is not exhausted by anyone's present understanding of it. . . . It would be a mistake to think that husbands and wives today have no more responsibility to and for one another than did married people in Old Testament times.

Precisely for the sake of marital love's growth, we must not attempt to define it in positive terms. To say, once for all, what marital love is and must be, would be to mummify it. Yet if married people have no way of identifying authentic love, they cannot pursue and foster it. Thus marital love is "defined" negatively, in terms of *exclusive* and *permanent* rights, mutually given and received, to marital acts. Thus, negative moral norms which absolutely exclude divorce (with remarriage) and adultery hold open the way for the constant growth and creative newness of marital love.

Remove the moral absolutes which make marital love possible without delimiting its possibility. Marital love will then be defined positively, in terms of certain skillful performances . . . , psychological satisfactions . . . , or social advantages. . . . Even if people succeed in pursuit of such goods, they will only complete projects, not receive a continuous and inexhaustible gift.

Maintain these absolutes and others like them. Human self-realization and progress have content which can generate operative

53. See Thomas Aquinas, *Commentary on Paul's Epistle to the Romans* c.13 lect. 2 ("praecepta negativa obligant semper et ad semper. Nullo enim tempore est furandum et adulterandum"); *In sent.* 3 d. 25, q.2, a.1b ad 3; *In sent.* 4 d. 17, q.3, a.1d ad 3; *Q.D. de Virt.* 3 (*De correctione fraterna*) a.1c and ad 4 (and see obj. 4, citing Rom. 3:8); *De malo* q.7 a.1 ad 8; *Summa Theol.* 2–2 q.33 a.2c; q. 79 a.3 ad 3. It should not be assumed that all negative norms are absolutes; the point is that all affirmative norms are nonabsolute.

[that is, specific] norms. These do not ideologically define a this-worldly goal, historically and culturally conditioned and constantly changing. But they do direct one to the service of the various goods of the person, to reverence for persons, and to preparing the material for the Kingdom [*Gaudium et Spes* 38 and 39]. Conforming to moral absolutes, one sometimes will pay the price of not effecting certain goods or of suffering certain evils. But one may confidently hope that God's re-creative act will respond to one's faithfulness.[54]

The philosophical and theological underpinnings of all this are explored in the following chapters. But I should not conclude my remarks about the stability of the nature of human fulfillment without recalling something else which Grisez elaborates.[55]

A moral absolute such as that excluding adultery is indeed to be understood as a requirement of human reason and nature. But it is not deduced by us from a prior knowledge of human nature. Rather, it discloses to us a form of human fulfillment and thus an aspect of human nature. Moreover, it is essential to the revelation of *God's* nature. Unless God had created sex, and thus familial relationships, we could not begin to understand the meaning of "Father," "Son," Trinity, Incarnation, and adoption as children of God. By its utmost intimacy which yet preserves the individual identities and roles of those who share it, marriage (defined by negative moral absolutes in the way Grisez recalled) discloses the possibility of divine-human communion, initiated by a covenant-relationship to which we trust God will remain faithful unconditionally, exceptionlessly, by a commitment which has the moral necessity and stability of absolute moral norms.

9. Rejection: some motivations and implications

What, then, is driving the rejection of the truth of moral absolutes? Bad arguments, many of which I shall discuss. But

54. Germain Grisez, "Moral Absolutes: A Critique of the View of Josef Fuchs, S.J.," in *Anthropotes* 1985/2, 176–77. For the definition of marriage, see *Code of Canon Law* (1983) canon 1056; see also 1134.
55. Loc. cit.

they are so many, and so poor, that one cannot but speculate about other motivations. These seem easy enough to find and understand. Pastoral considerations: lightening the burden when norms are conceived of—not as truths about service of goods which will be found again, transfigured, in the final Kingdom—but as laws imposed on freedom by fiat in the interests of some divine obstacle race, with rewards dubious (if any) and related merely extrinsically to the content of one's choices (IV.1); personal considerations: we all are sinners and would like to consider ourselves not so; the Enlightenment psychopathology of progress illustrated earlier (I.7); and, in general, a loss of the sense that revelation was completed in the life, the words, and the deeds of Jesus, communicated to and handed on by the apostles as a gospel which is "the source of all saving truth and all moral teaching" and "includes everything which contributes to the holiness of life . . . of the People of God."[56]

This last is fundamental. To affirm that Bentham, Mill, Marx, and, in his different way, Machiavelli were right in their rejection of the moral absolutes, and that the whole People of God was wrong until yesterday in accepting them as truths integral to salvation (ultimate and integral human fulfillment itself), and that the church's magisterium is wrong in proclaiming their truth to this day, is to take a long step toward denying that God has revealed anything to a people, or ever constituted a people of God at all.

56. See Vatican II, Dogmatic Constitution on Divine Revelation *Dei Verbum* paras. 4, 7, and 8.

CHAPTER II

Clarifications

1. *Intrinsece mala:* acts always wrong, but not by definition

Philosophical and theological reflections on moral absolutes have a history, illuminated by the tale, or tales, of the tyrant's wife. My version starts with Aristotle.

There seem to be two relevant texts in the *Nicomachean Ethics.* Having defined right actions and emotions in terms of a mean, intermediate between excesses, Aristotle adds:

> But not every action nor every passion admits of a mean; for some have names that already imply badness, e.g. spite, shamelessness, envy, and in the case of actions adultery, theft, murder. . . . It is not possible, then, ever to be right with regard to them; one must always be wrong. Nor does goodness or badness with regard to such things depend on committing adultery with the right woman, at the right time, and in the right way, but simply to do any of them is to go wrong.[1]

A characteristic midtwentieth-century academic interpretation is offered by the Oxford philosopher W. F. R. Hardie. Aristotle, he says, is making

> a purely logical point which arises from the fact that certain words are used . . . with the implication, as part of the meaning of the word, that [certain determinations within a range of action or passion] are excessive or defective, and therefore wrong. Thus . . . it does not make sense to ask when murder is right because to call a killing "murder" is to say it is wrong. . . . This, and no more than this, is what Aristotle means.[2]

---

1. *Nicomachean Ethics* 2.6: 1107a9–17 (trans. Ross-Ackrill-Urmson).
2. W. F. R. Hardie, *Aristotle's Ethical Theory* (Oxford University Press, 1968) 137.

There are theologians who assert (I do not say argue) that the Decalogue, too, contains no substantive, specific moral teaching; it merely exhorts us, through "formal" or tautologous formulations, to abstain from whatever we know on other grounds to be wrong: Do no wrongful killing, Do not have intercourse with the wrong person or on the wrong occasion, Do not take another's property when it would be wrong to do so.[3] A few, like John Dedek in the United States and Franz Scholz in Germany, have argued that the high medieval theologians, such as Albert and Thomas, equally proposed exceptionless norms only, or virtually only, in the uninteresting, formal sense: as norms specifying excluded acts by reference to vices or to unreasonable passions.[4] The affair of the tyrant's wife will show what we should think about that interpretation.

But first, back to Oxford. Hardie, you noticed, gives no argument to support his interpretation. Nor does he tell us just how to read the sentence "Goodness or badness with regard to such things does not depend on committing adultery with the right woman, at the right time, and in the right way." The parallel passage in Aristotle's *Eudemian Ethics*, which Hardie leaves unmentioned here, is even harder to read as making a merely logical point about the meaning of words: "A man is not an adulterer through having intercourse with married women more than he ought (there is no such thing): that is already a vice."[5]

3. See, e.g., Bruno Schüller, S.J., "Christianity and the New Man: The Moral Dimension—Specificity of Christian Ethics," in William J. Kelly, *Theology and Discovery: Essays in Honor of Karl Rahner S.J.* (Milwaukee, Wisc.: Marquette University Press, 1980) 307 at 309, 312.

4. John F. Dedek, "Intrinsically Evil Acts: An Historical Study of the Mind of St. Thomas," *Thomist* 43 (1979) 385 at 397, 399, 408–9; John F. Dedek, "Intrinsically Evil Acts: The Emergence of a Doctrine," *Recherches de Théologie Ancienne et Médiévale* 50 (1983) 191 at 225–26; Franz Scholz, "Problems on Norms Raised by Ethical Borderline Situations: Beginnings of a Solution in Thomas Aquinas and Bonaventure," in Charles Curran and Richard McCormick, S.J., *Readings in Moral Theology No. 1: Moral Norms and Catholic Tradition* (New York: Paulist Press, 1979) 158 at 168, 171, 173.

5. *Eudemian Ethics* 2.3: 1221b20–22; I use Michael Wood's translation (Oxford University Press, 1982), replacing his "seducing" with "having intercourse with" (Rackham; similarly Gauthier-Jolif) since the Greek *plesiazein* has not the morally pejorative overtones of "seduce."

In the same Eudemian passage, Aristotle remarks that when
people are accused of adultery, they admit to having sex with
a married woman but deny that it was adultery, pleading, for
example, that they were forced to—did it as a matter of necessity. And this question of compulsion or necessity (Aristotle
speaks of them here as if they were synonymous)[6] is the theme
of the other passage, in the *Nicomachean Ethics*, in which he
seems to touch on the question of moral absolutes.

There, in book 3, he is discussing passions and actions which,
being "involuntary," are the subject of pity and pardon rather
than praise or blame. He raises the question whether there is
involuntariness when one does "something base" (*aischron*, in
Latin *turpe*) "from fear of greater evils or for some noble object
(e.g. if a tyrant were to order you to do something base, having
your parents and children in his power, and if you did it they
would be saved, but otherwise they would be put to death). . . ."[7]
What are the "base" acts inculpably, even laudably, chosen for
some great and noble object? Aristotle's first commentator
whose work survives in any form, Aspasius (teaching in Athens
around 200 B.C.), opens a line of interpretation adopted nearly
fifteen hundred years later, and apparently independently, by St.
Thomas. What Aristotle had in mind, they suggest, did not
include acts which are morally bad (because excluded, they
imply, by some absolute moral norms), but only acts which are
ignominious—socially rather than morally shameful. Aspasius
offers an example: It would be right for a respectable man
to comply with a tyrant who threatens to destroy his city and
his family unless he goes about in public dressed like a
woman. . . .[8] And Aquinas offers two others: saving oneself

---

6. Cf. *Nic. Eth.* 3.1: 1110a1–2, b1–2 (*bia* and cognates) with 1110a27, 28, 32
and *Eud. Eth.* 1221b25 (*anagkazomenoi* and cognates); cf. *Metaphysics*
5.5:1015a23–b4.

7. *Nic. Eth.* 3.1: 1110a4–7.

8. Aspasius, in G. Heylbut, ed., *Aspasii in Ethica Nicomachea quae supersunt
commentaria. Commentaria in Aristotelem Graeca*, vol. 19 (1) (Berlin, 1889) 61 at
lines 26–29; Gauthier and Jolif, *L'Ethique à Nicomaque*, 2d ed. (Louvain: Publications Universitaires, 1970) 2:175.

from being burned to death, by telling a lie in jest or by undertaking some humiliating labor.[9]

The awkwardness of this interpretation makes very clear, by implication, the binding force which Aspasius and Aquinas attribute to the moral absolutes which they so conspicuously decline to (accept that Aristotle) set aside even in these desperate circumstances. But the issue was forced to explicitness by an ancient commentator, whom we know only as the anonymous Old Scholiast and date (insecurely) to the second century A.D.[10]

The Old Scholiast looks at Aristotle's problem with a different eye. He offers two examples of the acceptable "base acts": telling a lie for advantage (*pro utilitate*) and having intercourse with another's spouse in order to overthrow a tyrant.[11] You may find the latter suggestion vague; the Old Scholiast gives details in his commentary on book 5: here the picture is of seducing the tyrant's wife, so as to liberate the country.[12] How? The Scholiast gives no details, but a thousand years later St. Albert the Great, taking note of the Old Scholiast's position, suggests two possibilities. His suggestion when discussing *Nicomachean Ethics* book 2 is that by becoming familiar with the tyrant's wife, her seducer learns, and presumably forestalls, the tyrant's plans for pillaging the state.[13] In his commentary on book 5, he envisages

---

9. Aquinas, *In eth. III* lect. 2, n. 393: "aliquod turpe, non quidem peccatum, sed ignominiam aliquam"; also n. 394: "quaedam quae non oportet, non aliqua puta decentia ad statum suum . . . puta si alicui immineret sustinere ignis adustionem, nisi diceret aliquod iocosum mendacium, vel nisi aliqua vilia et abiecta opera faceret quae non decerent eius dignitatem."

10. See Anthony Kenny, *The Aristotelian Ethics* (Oxford University Press, 1978) 37.

11. Heylbut, ed., *Eustratii et Michaelis et Anonyma in Ethica Nicomachea Commentaria. Commentaria in Aristotelem Graeca*, vol. 20 (Berlin, 1892) 142: there are base acts not basely done: for lying is base, but it is not base to lie for advantage; and it is base to have sex (*misceri*) with a woman not your spouse, but not base to do so for the sake of overthrowing a tyrant; for baseness is in the choosing. . . .

12. Ibid. 249; Aquinas, *Opera omnia* (Leonine ed.), vol. 47(2) *Sententia Libri Ethicorum* (Rome, 1969) 324.

13. See Albert, *Opera omnia* (Aschendorff: Monasterii Westfalorum, 1972) 14,1, *Super Ethicam* p. 124 on *Nic. Eth.* 2,6:1107a12; also quoted by Gauthier in his introduction to Aquinas, *Opera omnia*, vol. 47(1) at 251*.

the seduction enabling the seducer to get close enough to kill the tyrant.[14] Details are still vague.

But of course they do not matter. The moral of this story, for us, lies in the reaction of the high medieval commentators to the Old Scholiast's implicit proportionalism. It was Robert Grosseteste, bishop of Lincoln, first chancellor of Oxford University, and perhaps the most substantial thirteenth-century English scholar, who introduced the Old Scholiast into the world of Latin Christianity. When he came to translate the Scholiast's comment on book 3, he broke out with one of his rare interjections:

The Christian religion declares and holds that sin must not be committed, whether for the sake of pursuing good (*utilitas*) or of avoiding loss. And so, since it is sin to lie and sin to have intercourse with another's wife (*alienae uxori misceri*), neither is in any way to be done. And so the teaching above is not doctrine but error, in the examples it proposes. For [and here he echoes the Vulgate of Romans 3:8] the evils of sin are not to be done for the sake of goods. . . .[15]

Albert the Great was equally blunt: "What the Commentator says is false";[16] "This saying of the Commentator is not true."[17]

St. Thomas, in one of his last writings, disposed of the whole matter with his usual economy and force, and in a way which flatly contradicts the claim that, for him (or his teachers or followers), "adultery," "fornication," "lying," "murder," and so on, are *defined* as wrongful. He intercepts and cuts off

---

14. Albert, *Opera omnia* 14,1, p. 380 on *Nic. Eth.* 5,10:1137b22 (also quoted by Gauthier in Aquinas, *Opera omnia*, vol. 47(1) 251*). Albert mentions the Old Scholiast's view on adultery also at p. 142, on 3,1:1110a19, but without any details.

15. See the Latin text in H. Paul F. Mercken, ed., *The Greek Commentaries on the Nicomachean Ethics of Aristotle*, vol. 1 (*Corpus Latinum Commentarium in Aristotelem Graecorum* 6,1) (Leiden: Brill, 1973) 239. See also ibid. 57* for Grosseteste's similar *notula* on 1110a1.

16. *Opera omnia* 14,1, p. 381 (on *Nic. Eth.* 1136b15–1137a30): "Commentator falsum dicit." Albert then suggests, hopefully, that the Commentator may have been speaking *civiliter* of an action *non dignus civili poena*.

17. Ibid. 142 (on *Nic. Eth.* 1110a19–29): "ad dictum Commentatoris dicendum, quod ipse loquitur secundum opinionem aliorum, et non est verum." Likewise p. 125: adultery can never be well done, and so the Commentator here speaks according to the opinions of "others."

any such misunderstanding by making an objector argue as follows:

Whatever is intrinsically sinful may not be done for any purpose however good—as Paul says in *Romans* 3:8. . . . But as the Commentator on the *Ethics* says, a morally good man commits adultery with the tyrant's wife, so that the tyrant may be killed and the country liberated. Therefore adultery is not intrinsically wrong, still less any other act of fornication.[18]

And his reply? "The Commentator is not to be followed on this matter; for one may not commit adultery for any good . . . ['pro nulla enim utilitate debet aliquis adulterium committere . . .']"[19] Note: Aquinas does not say that the objector's statement "Adultery is not intrinsically wrong" is nonsense, as it would be if adultery were *defined* as wrongful sex. Rather, Aquinas insists—and elsewhere argues—that adultery, defined as sex with another's spouse, is always wrong, whatever the circumstances.

I have labored over this story because of drastic confusions recently introduced by those who deny the truth of moral absolutes. They claim that the tradition, or the high tradition, did not teach absolutes but only tautologies such as, Wrongful sex is wrong and always to be avoided. Or they themselves (in tones of injured innocence)[20] deny that their proportionalist theory could ever permit adultery, fornication, lying, or murder! All this is entirely inconsistent with the tradition's manner of speaking. Nowhere in the tradition are any of these types of act *defined* as the proportionalist defines them, namely, as "wrongful sex," "disproportionate killing," "deceiving without good reason," and so forth. Everywhere in the tradition— not excluding Aristotle, in my view—these acts, though believed to be wrongful, are defined in such a way that their

18. *De malo* q.15 a.1 arg. 5 [4].
19. *De malo* q.15 a.1 ad 5 [4].
20. See, e.g., Richard A. McCormick, S.J., *Notes on Moral Theology 1981 through 1984* (Washington, D.C.: University Press of America, 1984) 3, 59, 64, 66.

wrongfulness is left logically open and is settled only by a further, nondefinitional judgment.

Of course, the force of this further, condemnatory judgment is sometimes so great that people are reluctant to allow the logically open question of wrongfulness to be raised. Following common idiom, people are willing to raise the question whether lying or suicide are justified, less willing to allow the question of extramarital sex to be posed as a question about the permissibility of "fornication" or "adultery," and distinctly unwilling to debate the question whether there are justified "murders." In the last-mentioned case, the condemnation of intentionally killing innocents has flowed backward into the common meaning or working definition of murder, and this backflow has been reinforced by the use of the term *murder* to express the verdict in criminal trials, and in general to sum up the allocation of morally or legally borderline cases of homicide between the moral or legal categories: thus, justified or excusable homicide is called "not murder," and wrongful homicide is called "murder." But in the high tradition which the proportionalists reject, the question whether murder (*homicidium*) can be justified is open, logically, just like the question whether suicide, lying, or extramarital sex (adultery, fornication) is ever justifiable.[21]

In short: The moral absolutes of the tradition of faith and of philosophy are not tautologies. They are not merely "formal" norms.

2. Specified neither evaluatively nor physically/behaviorally

Should we say, then, that they are "material" norms? Should we say that the acts they exclude, since not defined in morally

---

21. In other words, it is simply false to say that, in the tradition, terms such as "adultery" or "fornication" invariably "contain their own negative moral value judgment" or are "already defined to be morally wrong" (so that the proposition "adultery is wrong" is a tautology) as is regularly asserted by Richard McCormick, S.J., e.g. in his *Notes . . . 1981 through 1984* 64, 166.

evaluative terms, are defined in terms of "behavior," of "physical acts"? Those who deny that the tradition's absolutes can be true use this terminology to describe the norms they are contradicting. But it should be rejected out of hand.

For in these moral absolutes, the acts excluded from conscientious deliberation and choice are never defined in terms of behavior or physical acts, as such. Always these acts are described, as *Reconciliatio et Paenitentia* recalled, *ex objecto*, that is, in terms of the acting person's object: what that person chooses.[22] The norm expresses a moral judgment, not on physical or psychosomatic behavior as such, but on what is done just insofar as it expresses the acting person's will, a willing by which the acting person somehow relates himself or herself to the human goods at stake.

Aquinas puts the point starkly when he says that a conjugal act of intercourse and an act of adultery are *acts* of different types, even though the behavior, the physical and psychosomatic activity, may be identical.[23] And he does not mean to make the merely logical, empty point that the two types are morally *right* and morally *wrong*. Rather, he is saying that the reason why there can be this profound moral difference is precisely that, despite their physical identity, they are different types of human act: the wills of the parties relate to the human goods at stake in intercourse quite differently.

And so it is with all the moral absolutes in dispute. The physical behavior and causality and outcome can be exactly the

22. John Paul II, *Reconciliatio et Paenitentia* para. 17 (*Acta Apostolicae Sedis* 77 [1985] 185 at 221–22): "some sins are *intrinsically* grave and mortal by reason of their matter. That is, there exist acts which, *per se* and in themselves, independently of circumstances, are always seriously wrong by reason of their object. These acts, if carried out with sufficient awareness and freedom, are always gravely sinful. This doctrine, based on the Decalogue and on the preaching of the Old Testament, and assimilated into the kerygma of the Apostles and belonging to the earliest teaching of the Church, and constantly reaffirmed by her to this day. . . ."

23. *Summa Theol.* 1-2, q.18, a.5 ad 3; see also q.1, a.3 ad 3; *De malo* q.2 a.4c.

same, when completely different human acts are done.[24] A doctor who gives pain-killing drugs to relieve pain, aware that they will also shorten life, does an act quite different from that of the doctor who gives precisely the same drugs in order to hasten death and thereby eliminate pain. And there are many similar examples.[25] Equally, acts can be identical in every way relevant to a moral absolute's nonevaluative act-description, even though the physical behavior differs very noticeably. Thus, in the early 1960s, it was not those who understood and defended the tradition but those who were in the process of becoming proportionalists who argued that the *behaviorally different* features of the pill differentiated it from contraception (see IV.1). They have carried over their serious misunderstanding of the tradition's moral methodology into the years, since then, of their open

24. See further III.2. This consideration explains why Aquinas sometimes says that God can dispense from the Decalogue and sometimes (in the same works) says that God cannot. Insofar as the Commandments consist of formulations which can be taken as dealing with behavior which is *conventionally* defined as murder, adultery, and so on, or which is *behaviorally* (physically) the same as murder or adultery defined *ex objecto* (i.e., in terms of intentions and choices), they *can* be dispensed from by God, since his special mandate so changes the circumstances that the chooser's intention, the *object* of the act, can be different from what it is in all other cases to which the behaviorally or conventionally specified norm applies: cf. *In sent.* 1 d.47 q.1 a.4; *In sent.* 4 d.33 q.1 a.2; *De malo* q.3 a.1 ad 17. But when the Commandments are considered as they should be, as propositions bearing on human acts understood in terms of their precise intentionality (*ex objecto*), they are altogether exceptionless and cannot be dispensed from by God: *In sent.* 3 d.37 a.4; *Summa Theol.* 1-2 q.100 a.8; see also *De malo* q.15 a.1 ad 8. For this interpretation, see Patrick Lee, "Permanence of the Ten Commandments: St. Thomas and His Modern Commentators," *Theological Studies* 42 (1981) 422–43.
25. E.g., the physical behavior and causality and outcome can be *exactly the same* in (1-a) a case of shooting, foreseen as lethal, as the only available means of self-defense as in (1-b) a case of shooting to kill, chosen to take advantage of circumstances which will support the legal defense/excuse called "self-defense"; or in (2-a) a case of hysterectomy to deal with a uterine disease as in (2-b) a case of hysterectomy of the same uterus to prevent a possible future pregnancy; or in (3-a) a case of washing out the uterus with a spermicidal solution to repulse a rapist's invasion of a woman's body as in (3-b) a case of washing out the same uterus with the same spermicide to prevent pregnancy as a result of intercourse to which the woman consented. And so forth. In each pair, the relevant exceptionless moral norm identifies the excluded act in such a way as to exclude case (-b) while not excluding case (-a). Such norms, therefore, cannot relate merely to physical or material behavior, as such.

rejection of it. The resultant confusion in their discussion of the tradition, and in the writings of their students, is striking and frustrating.

It must be recognized that explanations of the tradition offered during the past century have given some encouragement to the misunderstanding. I am thinking of the distinction between *finis operis* and *finis operantis*, which Aquinas did not employ in the manner much later adopted. I am thinking, too, of certain explanations of the phrase "direct killing" or "direct sterilization" in terms of physical or causal immediacy, whereas the church's magisterium has constantly repeated the essential point: *direct* in this context means simply "as an end or as a means".[26]

In short: To define an act for the purposes of moral evaluation, one should look not to the physical behavior and causality precisely as such. Instead one should look to the proposal, combining envisaged end with selected means, which the acting person adopts (or may adopt) by choice, the proposal which any relevant behavior will express and carry out.

3. Opposed to reason and integral human fulfillment

Once it is clear that the moral normativity, the directiveness, of the moral absolutes is not smuggled in with the description of the excluded type of act (II.1), the question obviously arises, How, then, can such norms be true? What is the source, the explanation of their moral normativity? I have argued (I.4–6)

26. Thus "direct" killing of the innocent is explained as killing either as an end or as a means, by Pius XII (12 November 1944: *Discorsi & Radiomessagi* 6, 191–92), by Paul VI (*Humanae Vitae* [1968] footnote 14, and by the Congregation for the Doctrine of the Faith (*De Abortu Procurato*, 18 November 1974, para. 7; *Donum Vitae*, 22 February 1987, footnote 20). For similar explanations of "direct" in terms of "as an end or as a means," see: Pius XII, *Acta Apostolicae Sedis* 43 (1951) 838 (killing), 843–44 (sterilization); *Acta Apostolicae Sedis* 49 (1957) 146 (euthanasia); *Acta Apostolicae Sedis* 50 (1958) 734–35 (sterilization). On the question of craniotomy, see John Finnis, "Intention and Side-effects," in R. G. Frey and C. Morris, eds., *Liability and Responsibility* (Cambridge University Press, 1991) chap. 3 n. 34; Germain Grisez, *Christian Moral Principles* 309 n. 5.

that their normativity is not derived from their own effectiveness for results, and that effectiveness for results is not the criterion by which the moral judgments expressed in them identify acts or options as wrong or not wrong. But if effectiveness for results is not the criterion of moral rightness, what is?

We do not come to know, and cannot adequately explain, the truth and normativity of any moral principle or norm by reasoning from the nature of things (including human nature) just as such. Such conclusions cannot have terms (such as "morally ought") which are not in their premises.[27] For the same reason, we do not come to know any moral principle's truth and normativity from a knowledge of God's will considered simply as a fact about what God has chosen and commanded. The proportionalists are right in thinking that moral directiveness is essentially a matter of truths about the relationship between the activity directed and human good, well-being, fulfillment. But their account of the relationship between human good and morally significant choice is grossly oversimplified and incoherent (see I.6, II.3–5). It may be helpful, then, to summarize some results of work in basic ethical theory which I and others have undertaken, and which we continue to undertake and develop. This work is, in some respects, a strictly philosophical enterprise. But it is undertaken in the hope that whatever philosophically valid results emerge from it may help the theological enterprise of more adequately understanding, and following, the truths of the deposit of faith.[28]

Moral norms, like any other practical principles and norms,

27. See John Finnis and Germain Grisez, "The Basic Principles of Natural Law: A Reply to Ralph McInerny," *American Journal of Jurisprudence* 26 (1981) 21 at 22–25; John Finnis, "Natural Inclinations and Natural Rights . . ." in Elders and Hedwig, *Lex et Libertas* (1987) 43–49.

28. For what follows in this section, see the much fuller treatment and bibliography in Germain Grisez, Joseph Boyle, and John Finnis, "Practical Principles, Moral Truth, and Ultimate Ends," *American Journal of Jurisprudence* 32 (1987) 99–151. This article also gives a substantive reply to the critics who have claimed that this conception of ethics errs by departing from an "Aristotelean-Thomistic" "natural law" theory which we think is in fact quite unfaithful to Aquinas and, more important, rationally indefensible.

provide intelligent and rational guidance toward choice and action. They do so by identifying some intelligible good or goods which one can instantiate (make actual) and participate in by right action and spoil or miss by wrong action.

"Intelligible goods": There are many objects of human interest, but many of them make sense only as instrumental to, or parasitic on, the realization of other, more basic purposes and benefits. By reflectively analyzing human volitions—one's own and other people's—with their intelligible objects, one can uncover a number of basic purposes, basic benefits of human action, basic human goods. Each of these is an irreducible aspect of the fulfillment of human persons and is instantiated in inexhaustibly many ways in the lives of human persons.

These basic human goods correspond to the inherent complexities of human nature, as it is manifested both in individuals and in various forms of community. As animate, we are organic substances. Human life itself, in its maintenance and transmission, health and safety, is one category of basic good. As rational, we can know reality and appreciate beauty and whatever intensely engages our capacities to know and to feel. Knowledge and aesthetic experience are another category of basic good. As simultaneously rational and animal, we can transform the natural world by using realities, beginning with our own bodily selves, to express meanings and serve purposes. The realization for its own sake of such meaning-giving and value-creation is another category of basic good: some degree of excellence in work and play.

Each of these substantive basic goods is shared in by each of us, as a gift of nature and part of a cultural heritage, even before we understand them as goods and, as understood, begin to foster them, enhance them, and hand them on to others. But there are other basic goods which are only instantiated through the choices by which one acts for them. These reflexive basic goods correspond to that dimension of our reality whereby we are acting persons, acting through deliberation and choice. Not all instantiations of these reflexive goods are morally good, though true and lasting fulfillment in them must be.

Most obvious among the reflexive goods are various forms of harmony between and among individuals and groups of persons: living at peace with others, neighborliness, friendship. But within each of us, in one's personal life, similar goods can be realized; for feelings can conflict among themselves and can also be at odds with one's judgments and choices. The good opposed to such inner disturbance can be called inner peace. Again, one's choices can conflict with one's judgments and one's behavior can fail to express one's inner self. The corresponding good of harmony among one's judgments, choices, and performances is peace of conscience, with consistency between one's self and its expression. Finally, there is the peace which overcomes the tension which everyone who is alive to reality experiences in relation to reality's wider reaches and its depths: peace with whatever more-than-human source of reality, meaning, and value one can discover.

Such an outline of human fulfillment suggests many tempting philosophical questions. But the question directly relevant here is, Given the inexhaustible fields of opportunity which one identifies by identifying these open-ended basic human goods, how can anyone go wrong? What makes some things right and others wrong?

The basic human goods, taken with factual possibilities, delimit the range of *intelligent* action; anything one does which does not somehow instantiate one of those goods is pointless. But one does not go wrong by limiting one's actions to the intelligent, nor by choosing here and now to pursue only one or a few of the basic goods, and not others; that too is a limitation which, so far from being unreasonable, is actually required by reason. Where one does go wrong is by choosing options whose shaping has been dominated by *feelings*, not feelings which support or are in line with reasons (as *every* reasonable action must be somehow emotionally supported), but feelings which are calling the tune, not to the extent of swamping free choice and determining one's action but rather by impairing the rational guidance of action, fettering one's reason, limiting its directiveness, and harnessing it as feeling's ingenious servant.[29]

Feelings, for example, of egoism or partiality lie always await, ready to put reason to work devising rationalizations for one's unfairness. Against them, unfettered reason—the reason which, as Justin Martyr observed[30] earlier though less memorably than Augustine, loses many of its most disabling fetters when one is victim or onlooker—acknowledges a principle, the Golden Rule: Do to others as you would have them do to you.[31]

Again, hostile feelings such as anger and hatred toward oneself or others shape choices and actions which are often called "stupid," "irrational," or "childish" but are more accurately described as self-destructive or spiteful or vengeful. They destroy, damage, or block some instantiations of basic human good, in the interests of a feeling which harnesses reason to pursue a counterfeit of the basic human good of inner peace, a counterfeit because reason is being brought into line with feelings rather than feelings into harmony with reason and with the intelligible goods which give reason its content. Against such a feeling, unfettered reason acknowledges another principle: Do not answer injury with injury.

Thus we can begin to see the genesis of moral principles. They identify, and direct one away from, ways of cutting back on being fully reasonable.[32] But reason, here, does not mean some

29. There is no adequate way in English to refer to motivations, consequent upon sensory cognition, which are generically common to human beings and brute animals. Motivations of this sort normally are effective without one's being aware of them. So *feeling* and *emotion* have unwelcome connotations of conscious experience and intensity. But for want of better words, I use these, and use them interchangeably and as synonymous with the more old-fashioned word *passions*.

30. *Dialogue with Trypho* 93.

31. See Augustine, *Enarratio in Psalmum LVII* 1 (e.g., Henry Paolucci, ed., *The Political Writings of St. Augustine* [Chicago: Henry Regnery, 1967] 153–55).

32. "Moral truth as a kind of practical truth is not differentiated from moral falsity by the addition of any intelligibility other than the intelligibility proper to practical knowledge as such. Rather, *moral truth is differentiated by the integrity with which it directs to possible human fulfillment* insofar as that can be realized

formal structure of the mind, but rather one's practical knowledge of the intelligible basic human goods, understanding of which affords the starting-point for all deliberation and action which is not pointless. Thus, to say that immorality is constituted by cutting back on, fettering, reason by feeling is equivalent to saying that the sway of feelings over reason constitutes immorality by deflecting one to objectives not in line with *integral human fulfillment*, with the good of all persons and communities.[33] In other words, the first and most abstract principle of morality could be formulated: In voluntarily acting for human goods and avoiding what is opposed to them, one ought to choose and otherwise will those and only those possibilities whose willing is compatible with integral human fulfillment.[34]

---

by carrying out choices. Thus, moral falsities—for example, 'That so-and-so should be wiped out' and 'One must look out for number one'—are specified by the incompleteness due to which they lack adequacy to possible human fulfillment insofar as that can be realized by carrying out choices. . . . In the moral domain truth is the whole, and falsity a part, abstracted from the whole and thereby made to rationally guide action in a misguided way, just as if the part were itself the whole." Grisez, Boyle, and Finnis, "Practical Principles," 125–26.

33. Cf. Paul VI, *Populorum Progressio*, Encyclical Letter on the Development of Peoples, 26 March 1967, paras. 14–17 (*Acta Apostolicae Sedis* 59 [1967] 264–65: "To be authentic, development must be integral; that is, it must promote the good [*profectui*] of every man and of the whole man. . . .This fulfillment of the human person is not something optional. Just as the whole of creation is ordained to its Creator, so rational beings should of their own accord orientate their lives to God, the first truth and the supreme good. Thus it is that human fulfillment [*personae humanae profectus*] may be considered a *summa* of our responsibilities. . . . But each man is a member of society and thus belongs to mankind in its universality. So it is not just this or that individual, but all, who are called to promote the full development of human society in its entirety." See also Vatican II, *Gaudium et Spes* 35: "The norm of human activity is this: that in accord with the divine plan and will, it should harmonize with [*congruat*] the genuine good of humankind, and allow [*permittat*] men as individuals and as members of society to pursue and fulfill their integral vocation." See Grisez, *Christian Moral Principles* 183–89, 196–98. Note that neither Vatican II nor Paul VI proposes the *good of humankind* as a kind of *goal* to be attained by some sort of million-year plan.

34. On this first moral principle, see John Finnis, Joseph Boyle and Germain Grisez, *Nuclear Deterrence, Morality and Realism* (Oxford and New York: Oxford University Press, 1987) 281–84. In reflecting on this abstract formulation of morality's first principle, one will bear in mind the remarks of Alasdair MacIntyre, *Whose Justice? Which Rationality?* (Notre Dame, Ind.: Notre Dame University Press, 1988) 174–75: "It is a Cartesian error, fostered by a misunderstanding of Euclidean geometry, to suppose that first by an initial act of apprehension we can comprehend the full meaning of the premises of a deductive

Integral human fulfillment, then, is the ideal of practical intelligence and reasonableness working unfettered by feelings which would deflect it from its full directiveness. Nothing less than integral human fulfillment answers to reason's full knowledge of, and will's full interest in, the human good in which one can participate by action. But integral human fulfillment is not a state of affairs which could be effected by human action; it is an ideal of community, of the fulfillment of all human persons in all the basic goods. It is an ideal of reason and good will.

But the principle which directs us to will only what is compatible with it is no mere "ideal." It is the fundamental principle of morality. It is, indeed, a moral absolute—not a specific moral absolute such as those now in dispute (I.1), but the most abstract and generic moral absolute. The moral principles excluding revenge by any means and unfairness in any form are, likewise, absolutes. They share in the exceptionlessness and force of morality's ultimate first principle. For they are nothing other than specifications of that first principle—make one's choices all compatible with integral fulfillment, undeflected by one's fears and aversions, one's competing and partial desires, and one's inertia—stating that principle's necessary implications in relation to the various forms of emotion which can so fetter and deflect reason (without overwhelming or submerging it) that one does not choose what is unrestrictedly intelligent and reasonable.

Already it is clear that the absolutes of morality have nothing to do with "absolutizing the particular human goods"[35] which

---

system and then only secondly proceed to inquire what follows from them. In fact it is only insofar as we understand what follows from those premises that we understand the premises themselves. . . . So in the construction of any demonstrative science we both argue *from* what we take, often rightly, to be subordinate truths *to* first principles ([Aquinas] *Commentary on the Ethics* [I, lect. xii]), as well as from first principles *to* subordinate truths. . . . The moral life [is] a journey toward the discovery of first principles as an end, the full disclosure of which is, in both senses of 'end', the end of that journey. . . ."

35. *Pace* Josef Fuchs, *Christian Ethics in a Secular Arena* (Washington, D.C.: Georgetown University Press; Dublin: Gill & Macmillan, 1984) 82; K.-H. Peschke, SVD., "Tragfähigkeit und Grenzen des Prinzips der Doppelwirkung," *Studia Moralia* 26 (1988) 101 at 106–7.

they protect from unfairness, vengefulness, or all the other forms of wrong and wrong-making feelings. Nothing is unconditional (absolute) in moral thought save the demand of reason itself.

4. Worse than suffering wrong

The absoluteness of the first moral principle, and of its necessary specifications in high-level principles such as the two just mentioned, was graphically captured by Plato's Socrates in the saying which he proposed, defended dialectically,[36] and gave witness to in his own life and death: "It is better to suffer wrong than to do it."

This saying, on its face, does not assert the existence or absoluteness (exceptionlessness) of any specific moral norms such as the norms against murder or adultery. On its face, the Socratic dictum says no more, though no less, than: Once an option has been identified as wrong, it must not be chosen and done, whatever one's feelings, one's reluctance, one's distaste, fear. On its face, then, the dictum seems to be compatible with a proportionalist ethic, which equally will insist that once the option promising proportionately more premoral good than alternatives has been identified, one (morally) must choose and do it, even if it involves great disadvantages to oneself, for these disadvantages are, of course, supposed to have been included in the weighing process which the proportionalist tries to undertake. If one of the disadvantages to oneself were that one would suffer injustice at the hand of others, as a result of choosing the proportionalistically assessed greater good, then suffering this wrong is better—that is, it secures the greater premoral good—than doing the wrong of not choosing the greater good. And so we find some proportionalist theologians saying, with Bruno Schüller, S.J., that the Socratic dictum is true. And they go on to underline its importance by stating that within proportionalism there is at least one specific moral absolute: Do not cause any-

36. See, e.g., *Gorgias* 508e–509d.

thing morally bad; for example, do not participate in anyone's morally bad (wrongful) action.[37]

But the Socratic saying is, in fact, not so simpleminded and hospitable. Consider one of the events in which Socrates himself lived out his own saying. Plato has him tell the story: "The Thirty [Tyrants] summoned me and four others to the Round Chamber and ordered us to go and fetch Leon of Salamis from his home for liquidation . . . their object being to implicate as many people as possible in their evil. . . . When we came out of the Round Chamber the other four went off to Salamis and arrested Leon, and I went home."[38] If the tyranny had not collapsed soon afterward, Socrates' refusal to help liquidate Leon would have earned him the same sort of wrong: death at the hands of political gangsters. Since he had every reason to anticipate that, his choice was indeed "to suffer wrong rather than do it."

And *this* choice is scarcely likely to be made by the proportionalist. True, the proportionalist is likely to agree that political killings are a bad thing, with bad further consequences, and that it is generally wrong to do them, especially if one is, anyway, a tyrant ruling in one's own interests. So, if invited by the Thirty Tyrants to participate in such a killing, the proportionalist will politely—very politely—decline. But then the Tyrants raise the stakes; they threaten him with death if he does not participate. Things now look different to the consistent proportionalist.

Being no coward, and believing that morality is a matter of reason, he may discount his personal fears and assign them little or no weight in his balancing. But his fundamental moral concern is that good states of affairs be effected and bad states of affairs avoided. So he will notice that the alternatives before him

37. Bruno Schüller, S.J., "Direct Killing/Indirect Killing" in Charles Curran and Richard McCormick, eds., *Readings in Moral Theology No. 1* 139–42 (where he mistakenly claims that this is an analytic truth); his "La moralité des moyens," *Recherches de Science Religieuse* 68 (1980) 205 at 210. See also Bruno Schüller, S.J., in Richard McCormick and Paul Ramsey, *Doing Evil to Achieve Good* (Chicago: Loyola University Press, 1978) 184–88.

38. *Apology* 32c–e.

are, on the one hand; I participate in one wrong, and, on the other hand, I do not participate in that wrong and there are, in consequence, two wrongs (the one to Leon, and the one to me). But two wrongs, two killings of innocents, is a worse state of affairs than one. So the consistent proportionalist is likely to conclude, It is better, and morally right, that I should participate in liquidating Leon. It is better, here, for me to do wrong than to suffer it.

Now Schüller desires to maintain at least one specific moral absolute taught by the tradition. The desire is admirable, but the price he pays is incoherence. His oft-stated confidence that proportionalism ("teleology") can and must have one specific moral absolute, "Do not participate in the wrong of another," is grounded on his failure even to pose squarely the issue I have just raised (an issue widely discussed in the recent English-language philosophy from which he claims support).[39] The up-shot of that discussion is clear: A proportionalist, even one who like Schüller holds that moral wrong is the worst type of evil, has no coherent ground for denying the maxim, Better one murder than two *murders*. Better to participate in ten murders than make a choice which one knows will directly result in a hundred *murders*.

At the root of the problem, once again, is proportionalism's confusion between serving human good and effecting human good. Attempting the latter is often a reasonable, indeed the only reasonable, way of doing the former. But not always. There are situations where to attempt to effect good states of affairs is to choose to destroy, damage, or block the only human good which one's act can itself affect, the only human person to whom one's chosen act itself relates. For such a situation, Socrates' words and deed have a moral: Instead of trying to effect the apparently

39. See, e.g., Thomas Nagel, *Mortal Questions* (Cambridge University Press, 1979) 61–62; Samuel Scheffler, *The Rejection of Consequentialism* (Oxford University Press, 1982) 2–5, 80, 89–90 (Scheffler's discussion identifies the issue squarely but mishandles it by groundlessly assuming that there is, in situations of morally significant choice, a "best available state of affairs" identifiable prior to moral judgment and choice).

greater good of helping liquidate Leon, he just chose to serve the good of the one person whom he would himself, intentionally, have helped to destroy, Leon; and he went home.

(And here one may add a further, down-to-earth reflection on the proportionalist temptation. Its proposed identification of the balance of net, overall premoral goods and bads is an impossible project. The Thirty Tyrants' regime collapsed quite unexpectedly. The effects of Socrates' choice to go home, like the effects of Thomas More's refusal to lie, still ripple on through history, today—and whether for good or ill, at least incalculably.)

What Socrates had uncovered in his famous saying is that morality is not a matter of comparing possible events or states of affairs and identifying the better. One's choosing is itself part of the world. From the viewpoint of a comparison of states of affairs, the state of affairs in which A wrongs B (that is, B suffers wrong from A) is symmetrical, identical in terms of premoral and moral goods, with the state of affairs in which B wrongs A (that is, A suffers wrong from B). What Socrates says, in effect, is, It makes all the difference in the world that I am A, that it is a question of *my* doing the wrong. But that difference utterly disappears in a consistent proportionalist analysis, even one which tries to give a special weight to moral goods.

A further symptom of proportionalism's confusion in presenting deliberation as a comparison of alternative futures is the following, of interest to logicians of intentionality. If proportionalism acknowledges, as it must, that acting persons and their choosings and doings are a part of any of the possible futures whose goodness it seeks to weigh up, proportionalism must acknowledge also that (on its own assumptions about the comparative assessibility of the value of states of affairs) the following state of affairs could well promise the greater good or lesser evil: I do Y, on proportionalist grounds, but thereafter repent and live according to a moral code such as the Decalogue as interpreted in the tradition. Yet such a state of affairs, though I can envisage it as a state of affairs, is simply not a coherent object of choice; for no train of deliberation can, without mere self-contradiction, conclude that Y would be the *right* thing for *me* to do provided that *I* thereafter regard it as the wrong thing to have done. The way one's options relate to the human goods at stake in them is simply not captured by the model of a comparison of the human goods embodied in alternative states of affairs.[40]

5. Proportionalist justifications: incoherent with rationally motivated free choice

Socrates, Plato, and Aristotle did not have to face explicitly elaborated proportionalist philosophical proposals. Nor did the tradition (though it certainly was aware of incipiently proportionalist thoughts: III.2). Since we do, we need to articulate a full range of reasons for rejecting such proposals.

The deepest and most conclusive of the philosophical reasons, though by no means the easiest to grasp, is that the proportionalist method is incoherent with its own ambition to guide free choices.[41]

Proportionalism offers to guide morally significant choice, by identifying which of two or more intelligibly appealing options is the morally right option. (It is not concerned primarily—and so the following counterargument is not concerned at all—with cases in which one simply gives in to feelings, against all the relevant reasons.) It proposes that the right option is that which promises more good (overall, net of bads) than the alternative options promise. It thus proposes to compare the alternative options in terms of some conception of good common to them; as Garth Hallett, S.J., says on behalf of the proposal, comparison is possible because there is some common denominator, in terms of which all the various intelligibly appealing features of the

---

40. For further discussion of the logical issues raised in this section, see John Finnis, *Fundamentals of Ethics* 112–20.

41. For a full elaboration of the following argument, see Finnis, Boyle, and Grisez, *Nuclear Deterrence* 254–60.

respective options can be said to have more or less *value*, in a sense of "value" which holds constant as one moves from feature to feature.[42] Thus, the option promising greater good will have *all* the "value" of any alternative option, *and some more*.

And here lies the incoherence of proportionalism's project. For if one option seems to a deliberating agent to offer *all* that the alternatives offer *and some more*, the alternatives simply fall away; they completely lose the intelligible appeal which made them rationally choosable options. If I want a house and am interested in *only* three factors, price, size, and proximity to school, and I find a house which is cheaper and bigger and closer to school than any alternative, other houses simply drop out of consideration (unless I start to be interested in something else about the possibility of purchasing them). Within my house-hunting project there is no longer a choice between intelligibly appealing options. Morally significant, rationally motivated choices, which proportionalism seeks to guide, are not and cannot be made in situations where the alternatives to option X have *nothing* intelligibly attractive which X does not have, and X has *everything* the alternatives have, *and some more*.

Most proportionalists, like Hallett, simply ignore this argument, even when they are discussing the very pages where it has been proposed as decisive.[43] A few philosophers have attempted a reply on behalf of proportionalism. Surely, they say, a proportionalist who has identified the option which promises most good can still choose an alternative out of selfishness.[44]

The objection misses the point. Proportionalism is not offered as merely some sort of device for overcoming backsliding and selfish subrational motivations. Nor is it the openly futile offer to

42. Garth Hallett, "The 'Incommensurability' of Values," *Heythrop Journal* 28 (1987) 373 at 376–78.

43. Ibid. 374.

44. Robert McKim and Peter Simpson, "On the Alleged Incoherence of Consequentialism," *New Scholasticism* 62 (1988) 349–52. For a full critique see Joseph Boyle, Germain Grisez, and John Finnis, "Incoherence and Consequentialism (or Proportionalism)—A Rejoinder," *American Catholic Philosophical Quarterly* 64 (1990) 271–77.

II.5   CLARIFICATIONS   53

identify the morally right option *after* one has identified other available options as immorally egoistic. It offers to identify the morally right choice among alternatives which all have some rational appeal. And the insuperable problem it faces is that if its method of identification could succeed, the rationally motivated choice it offered to guide would become unnecessary.

The fundamental reason why rationally motivated immoral choices are as possible as morally right choices is that the intelligible goods promised by alternative choosable options are not commensurable, do not have some common denominator. The sense in which life is a good is not univocally the sense in which truth and friendship are goods. The sense in which intentional killing is a harm is not univocally the sense in which the causing of death as a side effect, or death by nonhuman forces, is a harm. The alternative to univocity is not, as Hallett supposes,[45] equivocation but analogy. But even where one is comparing alternative instantiations of one and the same sort of good (with a view to morally significant action), the instantiations have incommensurably different goodness. For each instantiation is an aspect of some individual person's or persons' reality (including the reality of the person deliberating and acting).

Notice that the incommensurability which makes proportionalism irrational is incommensurability of the goods involved in *options*. States of affairs considered in abstraction from their origins, context, and consequences (for example, their relation to a choosing human will) can often be compared in value: a happy village five minutes before and five minutes after a devastating hurricane. And many other comparisons of value are possible. Moral good can be ranked higher than nonmoral, intelligible good higher than merely sensible good, basic good than instrumental, divine and human than animal, heavenly than earthly. More of the same can be compared with less of the same; a genocidal society is worse than a murderous individual; killing is worse than wounding. These and many other com-

45. *Heythrop Journal* 28 (1987) 373 at 375, 376.

parisons can be made and can make common speech sound proportionalist.[46] But all were made in the tradition of philosophy and faith which yet, after the most profound reflection on human good, choice, and morality, remained steadfastly non-proportionalist. For none of these sorts of comparison is the sort the proportionalist needs: a rational judgment, made prior to moral judgment and choice, and concerning the intelligible goods in the options available for choice.

6. The central case: intentional harm, always unreasonable

On what principle did Socrates judge that it would be wrong to help kill Leon? Plato does not say. Was it simply the injustice of unfairness? That would hardly suffice, if Socrates' own life and his family's fate were all at imminent risk. I think the most decisive principle underlying Socrates' judgment that killing an innocent man is wrong is the principle which may be expressed in the classic formula, Evil may not be done for the sake of good. The place of this formula in the tradition I shall discuss in III.2. Here I take "do evil" to include at least the following: every choice to destroy, damage, or impede a basic human good. Every such option, every such proposal for choice, must be shaped by reason-fettering feelings—of emotional desire for or emotional aversion from some state of affairs.

For: The proposed destroying, damaging, or blocking of some basic aspect of some person's reality provides, of itself, *a reason* not to choose that option—the reason constituted (in the way that all basic, noninstrumental, more-than-sensory reasons for action are constituted) by that aspect of that person's fulfillment. And that reason could reasonably be set aside, and the option reasonably adopted, only if one could, prior to choice, identify some rationally preferable reason *for* choosing that option: that is, some greater good involved in or promised by that option

---

46. See Finnis, Boyle, and Grisez, *Nuclear Deterrence* 261–67.

than is involved in and promised by the options which do not include that choice to destroy, damage, or block a basic human good. But, for the reasons I have briefly described, such a commensurating of goods is rationally impossible. (If it were possible, the situation would cease to be one of choice between rationally appealing alternatives, and there would remain no rationally motivated choice.) To be the subject of a morally significant choice, the option to destroy, damage, or impede a basic human good must have some rational appeal, must involve some intelligible goods. But the judgment that this option is rationally *preferable* must be based not on reason but on feelings—the *feeling of desire* for the goods which will be missed or the *feeling of aversion* from the bads which will be suffered if one does not choose that option—feelings which inspire the inevitably unreasonable conclusion that, on the balance of premoral goods and bads, to destroy, damage, or impede that basic human good will be the lesser evil and will yield greater good. When that conclusion is set aside as unreasonable, one is left with the basic human good immediately at stake in the option to destroy it intentionally, with the reason against such options which is entailed by the directiveness of the primary practical principles directing one toward such basic human goods and away from what destroys, damages, or impedes them.

Thus the principle that evil may not be done for the sake of good takes its place alongside the Golden Rule and the principle that injury is not to be met by injury. It is a further implication of the supreme principle that one's willing must be in every way compatible with integral human fulfillment, which is the content of practical reason's directiveness when that is not fettered or deflected by feeling.

7. Deadly defense and death penalty: not necessarily proportionalist

But an objection springs to mind. Surely the tradition accepted that one may rightly choose to kill, to destroy the life of a human being, for the sake of greater good, for example, to save a larger number of lives, or the life of a more important person?[47]

Aquinas, for one, did not think so. In this context, as in *all* others, he firmly denies that one should seek to identify, and choose, "the lesser evil."[48] Killing in self-defense, capital punishment, and public killings in war against external or internal enemies were none of them justified by him on any such ground. To show the possible justification of killing in self-defense, he used exclusively an analysis of action, distinguishing between intention and side effect.[49] To argue for the possible justification of killing in the administration of justice, he contended (in effect) that such a killing need involve no choice to destroy a human good either as end or as means, but instead can be done with a different intentionality, that is, under a different description: restoring the order of justice violated by the one killed who, moreover, by his violation of justice, his fault, had removed himself from the dignity of the human.[50] Here, I believe, Aquinas's explanation may be challenged. Still, his intent to avoid

47. Richard McCormick, S.J., places particular reliance on this objection, particularly on the tradition's acceptance of capital punishment; see, e.g., his *Notes . . . 1965 through 1980* 453, 506, 647, 811 n. 21. McCormick helps his objection along by resolutely ignoring the tradition's doctrine of the retributive rationale of punishment, a rationale very different from any use of punishment as a means (e.g., deterrent) to bringing about a better future state of affairs. When this is drawn to his attention (as by Finnis, *Fundamentals of Ethics* 128–30), McCormick replies by denying the "Christian sense" of a retributive rationale of punishment: "Notes on Moral Theology: 1984," *Theological Studies* 46 (1985) 50 at 52 n. 4. He omits to mention that the rationale is that which is advanced by St. Thomas and all Christian moralists down to our own day: *Summa Theol.* 1-2, q.87, a.6c; *Summa contra Gentiles* 3, c.140, para. 5; c.146, para. 1; Pius XII, "Discourse to Sixth Congress of Penal Law," *Acta Apostolicae Sedis* 45 (1953) 739ff.

48. In every context in which a moral issue is to be resolved, Aquinas refuses the invitation to solve the issue by identifying "the lesser evil": see *In sent.* 4 d.6 q.1 a.1 qa.1 obj.4 and ad 4 (killing); d.9 a.5 qa.1 obj.3 and ad 3; *Summa Theol.* 2-2, q.110 a.3 obj.4 and ad 4; 3 q.68 a.11 obj.3 and ad 3 (killing); q.80 a.6 obj.2 and ad 2.

49. *Summa Theol.* 2-2, q.64, a.7c.

50. 2-2, q.64, a.2; Lee, "Permanence of the Ten Commandments," 438–41; William E. May, "Aquinas and Janssens on the Moral Meaning of Human Acts," *The Thomist* 48 (1984) 566 at 594–95.

any explanation of the type which proportionalism uses and generalizes is very clear.

But what grounds the very precise conception of actions, choices, and intentions which is required for any clear understanding of "Evil may not be done for the sake of good?" That question proves to have an answer as much theological as philosophical.

CHAPTER III

Christian Witness

1. Free choice: a morally decisive reality

Everyone has the experience of choosing, and of constraints—physical and psychological, logical, cultural and social—which block choosing what one wants or doing what one chose. But outside the cultures formed by the Old and New Testaments, few have acknowledged with clarity or firmness the reality of *free choice*.

There is free choice where one really does have *motives* for choosing and doing each of two or more incompatible options, but these motives are not determinative, and neither they nor any other factor whatever, save the choosing itself, *settles* which alternative is chosen.

Because nothing—not even the motives which are necessary though not sufficient conditions for making the choice—settles the free choice, save one's own very act of making it, that act is truly creative. It is creative of personal character, and thus of a most significant aspect of the reality of each person who is capable of meaningful relations with other persons, human and divine, because capable of establishing some meaningful relationship between his or her feelings, understanding, judgments, and actions.

The transcendence of God to the created universe, the utter originality of the act of divine creation, and the independence of that act from every kind of necessitating condition are impossible for us to conceive save on the analogy of the human free choice. Conversely, only those cultures which proclaim divine creation and meditate on its significance display a firm grasp of the reality of human free choice. And, apart from that reality, interpersonal relationships such as those in the heavenly communion looked for by Christian faith are equally inconceivable. For the reflexive goods of friendship, inner tranquillity, authenticity, and love of God, are all constituted by free choices or the dispositions which such choices establish. It is no coincidence that the Enlightenment, which denied divine transcendence and causality and the hope of heaven, denied also the reality of free choice (I.6).

And denied specific moral absolutes. The profound inner connection between free choice and the tradition's specific moral absolutes is this chapter's theme. I shall not here defend the reality of free choice. But it is worth remarking that the incoherence in proportionalism (II.5) was first clearly identified, by Boyle and Grisez, in the course of elaborating their potent argument that the rational denial of free choice is self-refuting.[1]

2. Evil: not to be chosen that good may come

Some of Christian tradition's most decisive witnesses to the the truth of moral absolutes have been mentioned (I.2–3), particularly the Decalogue in its reaffirmation and paradigmatic interpretation by Jesus, so manifest in the Synoptic Gospels.[2]

John's Gospel, in which no word is at random, places before us, not once but twice, the rhetorical question of Caiaphas: "Is it not better that one innocent person be put to death than that the whole people perish?" (John 1:50; 18:14) The question is general. But since one particular person's fate hangs on the answer, the evangelist's careful articulation of the question, in that particular context, clarifies and powerfully reinforces the faithful

---

1. Joseph Boyle, Germain Grisez, and Olaf Tollefsen, *Free Choice: A Self-Referential Argument* (Notre Dame, Ind.: Notre Dame University Press, 1976) for a brief sketch of the main argument, see John Finnis, *Fundamentals of Ethics* (Washington, D.C.: Georgetown University Press, 1983) 137.

2. Especially Mark 10, Matt. 19, Luke 16 and 18.

reader's acknowledgment of the norm (and the underlying principle) embodied in faith's inevitable answer, No!

But John presents us also with another image: the man who not only, like Peter, offers to lay down his life for his friend (John 13:37), and not only describes laying down one's life for one's friends as the greatest of human acts of love (15:13) but actually himself, knowing all that was to befall him (18:4), and in fidelity to the mission for which he came into the world (18:37), accepts the great wrong (19:11) of crucifixion. The particular relevance of this image, this careful re-presentation of the reality of a particular human choice and act, consists in the distinction which it implicitly presupposes: between Jesus' choice (freely to accept death[3] without in any way joining his will with his accusers' sinful will) and any choice that could rightly be described as suicidal, as choosing, intending, one's own death.[4]

Some people, in the first ferment of belief in humankind's definitive redemption through Christ by grace, opined that wrongdoing is tolerable or even desirable because it affords occasion for God to accomplish his redemptive work: compare Romans 6:1 and verse 15. And as Romans 3:8 makes clear, some people actually claimed that St. Paul's own preaching of redemption carried that implication. The line of thought is developed quite clearly from verses 5 to 8:

(5) If our wickedness serves to show the justice of God, shall we say that God is unjust to inflict wrath upon us? (7) . . . if through my falsehood God's truthfulness abounds to his glory, why am I still being condemned as a sinner? (8) And why not do evil that good may come?—as some slanderously charge us with saying.

Human faithlessness (v. 3), unrighteousness, denials of the truth have a good side effect: they give God glory by affording the

---

3. "a death he freely accepted": *Roman Missal*, ICEL translation 1973, Second Eucharistic Prayer (translating *voluntarie*).

4. The comprehensive Christian rejection of suicide is well elaborated by Augustine, *De civitate Dei* 1, 17–27; exploiting for his own purposes the Roman love of role-models (*exempla*: see c.22, 2), Augustine's first move (in c.17) is to point to the suicide of Judas Iscariot.

opportunity of demonstrating his fidelity, holiness and truth-fulness. That good effect is surely greater than the evil in the actions! How then (v. 7) can God, in his final judgment on those actions, regard them as evil? Indeed, why should not those who notice this connection between their actions and God's glory pursue that greater good directly, by choosing to do what would otherwise be sin as a *means* of bringing about that greatest good?

Such is the general line of thought which Paul is concerned to display and reject. On this, there is impressive agreement by modern translators and exegetes. True, almost all modern ex-egetes leave the thought "Evil may be done for the sake of good" no further elaborated than: "antinomianism,"[5] "libertinism,"[6] *pecca fortiter.*[7] But their own agreement on the sequence of thought allows us to be more precise. This is antinomianism with a difference; it is a rejection of moral norms on the precise ground that to depart from them will yield, not merely what I happen to want here and now, but precisely an *intelligible* good which is *greater* than any bad (moral or nonmoral) involved in my action. The intelligible good in question in Romans 3:8 is God's glory. But Paul's brusque and total rejection of this line of thought entails certain conclusions.

5. E.g., Matthew Black, *Romans*, New Century Bible Commentaries (London: Marshall, Morgan & Scott, 1973) 62; W. S. Campbell, "Romans iii as a Key to the Structure and Thought of the Letter," *Novum Testamentum* 23 (1981) 22 at 35–36; Isaac J. Canales, "Paul's Accusers in Romans 3:8 and 6:1," *The Evangelical Quarterly* 57 (1985) 237 at 244; Raymond F. Collins, *Christian Morality: Biblical Foundations* (Notre Dame, Ind.: Notre Dame University Press, 1986) 246, 248; C. E. B. Cranfield, *A Critical and Exegetical Commentary on the Epistle to the Romans* (Edinburgh: T. & T. Clark, 1975) 186 n. 4; David R. Hall, "Romans 3.1–8 Reconsidered," *New Testament Studies* 29 (1983) 183 at 194; William Sanday and Arthur C. Headlam, *A Critical and Exegetical Commentary on the Epistle to the Romans* 4th ed. (Edinburgh, T. & T. Clark, 1900) 74; E. P. Sanders, *Paul, the Law and the Jewish People* (Philadelphia: Fortress Press, 1983) 31; Frank Stagg, "The Plight of Jew and Gentile in Sin: Romans 1:18–3:20," *Review and Expositor* 73 (1976) 401 at 411–12.

6. E.g., Ernst Kaesemann, *Commentary on Romans* (Grand Rapids, Mich.: Eerdmans, 1978), 85; Collins, *Christian Morality*, 246, 248.

7. J. A. T. Robinson, *Wrestling with Romans* (Philadelphia: Westminster Press, 1979), 34.

The first conclusion is that rightly drawn (as we shall soon see) by Augustine and (as we have seen: I.6, II.7) by Grosseteste, Albert, Thomas—and then by the entire Catholic moral preaching and theological tradition down to Pius XI in *Casti Connubii* (1930)[8] and Paul VI in *Humanae Vitae* (1968).[9] Since St. Paul does not dispute that sin brings about the incomparably great good of God's glory, his teaching entails that the question whether an act is wrongful is *not to be settled* by trying to show that in a given case it would bring about consequences greater in goodness, or lesser in evil, than the goods attained or evils avoided by alternative acts. *Nor* is it settled by showing that the act in question can be regarded as a part of some totality than which no greater created good can be conceived.

A second conclusion is this: One of the reasons why the first conclusion is justified is that the opposed, proportionalist view involves the intolerable paradox (I.4). Combined with Christian faith in providence, proportionalist moral method yields, willy-nilly, the all-purpose practical norm, Try anything. It seems to me that, in Romans 3:5–8, Paul was virtually articulating that implication and identifying it as what it is: a reductio ad absurdum of attempts to understand morality in terms of *effectiveness* (intended or actual) for good.[10]

We may conclude, third, that Grisez summed up the position accurately enough when he wrote, concerning Romans 3:8:

Proportionalists deny the relevance of this verse of St. Paul as a proof text against their position. They claim that Paul only excludes the choice of a moral evil, not of a premoral evil proportionalism seeks to justify.

---

8. The encyclical states that to justify a direct abortion by its consequences would violate "the divine precept promulgated in the words of the Apostle: *Evil is not to be done that good may come of it*": Acta Apostolicae Sedis 22 (1930) 541 at 564; Denz.-Schoen. 3721.

9. Para. 14; *Acta Apostolicae Sedis* 60 (1968) 481 at 491.

10. Robinson, *Wrestling with Romans* 34, observes that the same thought may well be discernible in Wisdom 15:1–2: "But thou, our God, art kind and true, patient , and ruling all things in mercy. For even if we sin we are thine, . . . ; but we will not sin, because we know that we are accounted thine." Robinson notes that the error in question is of confusing the moral relationship (of love of God and responsibility before him) with "the standpoint of a spectator." Cf. II.4.

However, the preceding verse is raising precisely the question whether what otherwise would be evil—a lie or refusal of truth—might not be justified if it promotes God's glory. Still, *I do not use Rom 3.8 as a proof text against proportionalism*, for without an *independent and conclusive critique* of proportionalism, its proponents could plausibly argue that Paul's rejection of violating truth to promote God's glory is a specific norm whose extrapolation into a general principle is question-begging.[11]

But, as we have seen, independent and conclusive critiques of proportionalism are indeed available. One of those is the theological critique, identifying the incoherence of proportionalist moral method with belief in providence (I.4). What is striking is how far that critique is anticipated by Paul's rapid critique of (what the exegetes now, too vaguely, call) "antinomianism."

St. Augustine knew as well as any modern exegete that Paul's primary concern in Romans 3:8 is not with any specific moral norm but with a precise though far-reaching argument for a wide-ranging "antinomianism."[12] But Augustine also saw that the logic of Paul's position tells against other arguments seeking to justify choices against a human good. The human good in issue in Augustine's treatises on lying is, of course, the good of truth—participation in truth through knowledge and communication of it.

Augustine's first treatise on lying, *De mendacio* (written about 395 A.D., before he became a bishop) is an extraordinarily ener-

11. *Christian Moral Principles* 168 n. 32 (emphases added). Giving a fine example of proportionalist manipulation, Raymond F. Collins, *Christian Morality: Biblical Foundations* 238, quotes the first three sentences but *omits* the fourth and immediately states, "In the exposition of his own position, Grisez unabashedly cites Rom 3:8 as a proof text or Scriptural warrant for the moral adage that the end does not justify the means"! The passages from *Christian Moral Principles* which Collins then cites each in fact take Rom. 3:8 to be supporting "the moral adage" (actually, that "we may not do evil that good may come of it": 155) by advancing quite specific lines of thought *derived from the context* of Rom. 3:8 (a context which, Collins insinuates, Grisez overlooked), viz. (i) that we do not have the same responsibility God has for the good he wills (155), and (ii) that Paul excludes rationalizations which would seek to justify evildoing for the sake of religion (220). Grisez's treatment of the passage is everywhere consistent with the exegetical learning assembled by Collins.

12. See, e.g., Augustine, *De fide et operibus* (circa 413) xiv, 21.

getic, and not wholly conclusive, philosophical and theological exploration of the most powerful arguments and examples which can be mustered to defend the rightness of "necessary lies." In it he confronts the opinion of "those who say that no deed is so evil that one ought not to do it to avoid a greater evil, and that what one does," that is, what one is responsible for, "includes not only what one actually performs but also what one willingly suffers," in the extended sense of "willingly" in which the martyr suffers death willingly rather than do wrong.[13] Augustine, in other words, knew the characteristic consequentialist (now we might say "utilitarian" or, similarly, "proportionalist") thesis that no act can be judged wrong unless one has weighed up the totality of its foreseeable consequences against the totality of foreseeable consequences of alternative available options— and that one's responsibility for the *side effects* of fidelity to a moral absolute often makes that fidelity paradoxical or morally foolish. We see again what we began to see in Paul: that the theological tradition's adherence to moral absolutes was made with an awareness of the alternatives.

Augustine's later work on lying, *Contra mendacium*, was written in 420 A.D., against the activities of Catholics who infiltrated heretical circles to discover and later denounce covert heretics. On the opening page, he formulates the core of his response: the zeal to eliminate heresy is admirable, but unearthing heretics by lying amounts to saying "Let us do evil that good may come," something "which you see how the Apostle Paul detested."[14] In developing his response, Augustine portrays with great frankness all the inner feelings and popular suasions which move him, like anyone else, to want to lie. In the storm of objections and temptations which he puts to himself, his life raft,

---

13. *De mendacio* ix, 12. This tract also contains his own formulation of the Socratic saying (see II.4): Although murder is worse than theft (by, for example, forging a will), committing theft is worse than being murdered (ix, 14). *Contra mendacium* ix, 22, contains the dictum itself: It is better to suffer wrong than to do it.

14. *Contra mendacium* i, 1; see also the echoes throughout 18 and very plainly in the penultimate sentence of xv, 32.

the consideration he judges will hold firm for all his Christian readers, is the moral absolutes against denial of faith, and adultery.[15] If the arguments defending lying as the lesser evil were valid and true, the same would have to be said of adultery.[16]

Thus something going far beyond the theological opinions of Augustine himself becomes clear. In the Christian community of his day, although there was confusion about lying, there was practical unanimity on two points, One may never do wrong in order to prevent a greater wrong.[17] And the norm excluding adultery (any choice of extramarital sexual intercourse involving one or more married person) is one of a number of exceptionless moral norms, identifying in nonevaluative terms a type of act which will always be wrong even when done to prevent great wrongs.

In the middle of Augustine's tract is the page of general moral theory (7, 18) which became foundational for Catholic moral theology from the thirteenth to the twentieth century. For when Peter Abelard, in the second quarter of the twelfth century, argued (ambiguously) that behavior is morally indifferent and the morality of acts depends entirely on intention and was understood or, perhaps, misunderstood as contending that there are no specific moral absolutes, the decisive reply was given, within a decade or two, by Peter Lombard (2 *Libri quatuor sententiarum* d.40). And the reply consists of a quotation of this passage from the *Contra mendacium*, together with the injunction to take it very seriously, and some sentences of paraphrase.

Intention and purpose, Augustine is here saying, are of great importance in judging acts good or bad. But there are some things, he immediately adds, which are clearly wrong and may not be done, not for any plea of good cause, for any seeming good end, for any supposedly good intention. These are *per se* wrongful. Examples are thefts, fornication, blasphemies, lies in

---

15. See xix-xxi, 40–41.   16. vii, 17.
17. See especially ix, 20–21.

the witness box, forgeries of wills so as to divert money to the
poor or ransom captives or build churches, playing gigolo to rich
women so as to give one's gains to the needy. In relation to
something wrongful (*malum*) *per se*, Lombard infers and says,
we should deny that its wrongfulness comes from purpose or
will (*ex fine et voluntate*, or *secundum intentionem et causam*).

With Lombard's last-mentioned view Aquinas disagrees, mag-
isterially, in his first work touching morals. His disagreement is
not with the judgment that there are acts which, as he states, are
wrong in themselves and cannot in any way be rightly done (*de
se malus, qui nullo modo bene fieri potest*). It is with Lombard's
denial that such acts are wrong by reason of will, intention,
purpose (*finis*). Such acts, says Aquinas, *are* wrongful by reason
of the acting person's will. There need be nothing wrong with his
intentio or *voluntas intendens*, his ultimate motivating purpose
(*finis ultimus*), for example, to give money to the poor. What is
wrongful is, rather, his choice, his *electio* or *voluntas eligens*, his
immediate purpose (*objectus proximus* or *finis proximus*), for
instance, to forge this testament.[18] The goodness or badness of
what Aquinas calls the "exterior act" (which signifies everything
one does to carry out one's choice, even what lies entirely within
one's own mind, as in sins of thought) depends entirely on the
goodness and badness of one's will, choice, immediate purpose,
that is, on what one chooses and tries to do, including what one
chooses and attempts as a means to one's ultimate purpose.[19]
From all this, though his later analyses are more complex, Aquinas will never deviate. The rightness or wrongness of behavior is
totally dependent on the rightness or wrongness of the deliberating and choosing which makes that behavior voluntary and thus
morally significant action of some specific sort.[20]

From Peter Lombard down to the Second Vatican Council, the
position so forcefully expressed by Augustine and so clearly
explained by the young Aquinas was peacefully accepted in

18. Aquinas, *In sent.* 2 d.40 a.2.   19. d.40 a.2c.
20. See John Finnis, "Object and Intention in Moral Judgments According to
Aquinas," *The Thomist* 55 (1991) 1–27.

Catholic theology.[21] I need not repeat the council's solemn articulation of the specific moral absolute against every act of "indiscriminate" bombing of cities, that is, bombing not intended exclusively to affect combatants and their operations. Here I shall simply recall the council's reflective restatement of the Socratic "Better to suffer than to do wrong." In *Gaudium et Spes* 27, having condemned various acts which "are opposed to life itself, such as homicide of every kind, genocide, abortion, euthanasia, and willful (*voluntarium*) suicide," together with other acts which violate the integrity of the person or human dignity, the council observes that such acts "do more harm [or: are more degrading, *inquinant*] to those who carry them out than to those who suffer the wrong."

3. Actions: morally specified by their objects (intentions)

Underlying these strategic Christian testimonies to the truth of moral absolutes are beliefs and dispositions which I have already emphasized—above all, trust in divine providence, and the distinction between the loving service of human good and the effecting of good states of affairs (I.4). I want now to reflect on something partly implicit, partly explicit, in these testimonies: the rejection of certain types of *choice* or *intention*.

The tradition teaches, as these witnesses show, that certain types of choice and intention are incompatible with love of God and with seeking the Kingdom, because incompatible with love

21. So Richard McCormick was really rejecting a central strand in the whole tradition in remarking that, when St. Thomas appeals to the axiom that good ends do not justify evil means, he "had to be referring to *morally* evil acts, as his use of the term 'lie' would suggest; or else Thomas needs correction": *Notes on Moral Theology 1965 through 1980*, 763. Aquinas's definition of *lie* (*mendacium*) is free of evaluative terms, i.e., does not presuppose that lying is morally evil; his statement that evil means are not justified by good ends is therefore not the empty "morally wrong acts cannot be justified," and therefore "needs correction" if it is to be brought into line with McCormick's proportionalism (which must treat Rom. 3:8 as empty, erroneous, or grossly misinterpreted by the tradition).

of human good. So: Whatever may be said about persons
who do such acts believing them to be justified, or without the
clear understanding that sufficient reflection would induce, such
choices and intentions must simply be excluded from one's own
deliberation and choice. Accepting death as a foreseen and humanly certain result of one's choice to remain faithful to one's
mission to save others can be spoken of as laying down one's life
for one's friends, but it is not an act of suicide, of intending to
kill myself (or of intending that others kill me) as a means to an
end (III.2). Killing noncombatants as a side effect, which one
clearly foresees and thus accepts, of one's properly motivated
military operations can be acceptable; but killing noncombatants, by the very same devices, as a means of demoralizing
enemy combatants or of impeding them with crowds of terrified
refugees is never to be intended, chosen, done.

This sort of distinction matters because free choice matters.
Let me indicate, first, how it is entailed by the reality of free
choice and, second, why free choice has the moral significance it
does.

Choice is between intelligibly appealing options. But an option is not yet the state of affairs one hopes to bring about by
action. Rather, an option is a *proposal* for action, and choice is
precisely the adoption of that proposal *rather than* alternatives.
Being intelligibly appealing, the proposal includes all, and only,
that which makes it seem worthwhile to attempt whatever one
will attempt in trying to carry out the proposal. Thus the proposal includes both one's "ultimate" purpose (say, restoring
one's health, giving expression to one's friendship, restoring
peace with justice) and all the means one judges appropriate to
effecting that purpose (taking bitter medicine, acquiring thus-
and-thus a gift to give one's friend, undertaking military operations thus-and-thus). The means are included in the proposal,
not under some description which makes them seem compatible
with some legal or moral rule but under that description which
makes them intelligibly attractive *as means*—that is, the description under which they enter into one's deliberation toward

choice (not one's rationalizing of attempts to square that choice with one's conscience or with the law). Thus, if one decides that such-and-such a military operation is needed in order to block the enemy's tank columns with crowds of refugees, and that the way to make noncombatants become refugees is to destroy or injure some of them in their homes, then killing or injuring noncombatants in their homes is intelligibly attractive and is the relevant true description of what one chooses and does. That description does not alter just because one tells oneself and others that what one is doing is "bombing military targets" in the sense of targets whose destruction will have an effect on military operations.

Choice, then, is of proposals, and the proposals one shapes in one's deliberations include one's ends and one's means. Deliberation is for the sake of action, and in one's acting every means one has adopted in one's proposal has the character of an end, something one must set out to achieve. So, everything included within one's proposal has the character of *end*, of purpose, of objective. The distinction between ends and means is only relative: all one's means are intermediate ends, subordinate objectives on the way to one's further end or ends, to the ultimate point, simple or multiple, of the choice and action.[22] To use the classical terminology of Thomas, used again in *Reconciliatio et paenitentia*, one's proposal, end and means (remote objective(s) and proximate objectives), is the *object* of one's choice and act.[23]

22. As Aquinas says in *De veritate* q.5 a.4 ad 11 [10] (in some editions, see the corpus of the article itself): "in the set of means to an end, all [means] intermediate [between the agent and the end] are ends as well as means [in ordine eorum quae sunt ad finem omnia intermedia sunt fines et ad finem, ut dicitur in II *Physica* (II,5:194b5) et *Metaphysica* V (V,2:1013a35)]." His commentaries on the *Physics* 2 lect. 5 (no. 181: "each intermediary between the prime mover and the last end is, in a way, an end [omnia quae sunt intermedia inter primum movens et ultimum finem, omnia sunt quodammodo fines] . . .") and the *Metaphysics* V (no. 771: "non solum ultimum, propter quod efficiens operatur, dicitur finis respectu praecedentium; sed etiam omnia intermedia quae sunt inter primum agens et ultimum finem, dicuntur finis respectu praecedentium . . .") give a vivid and careful illustration of this from medical practice.

23. "Considered as a certain state of affairs [res], the end is an object of the will different from the means, but considered as the reason for [and meaningful

If one is asked, or asks oneself, *what* one is choosing and doing, one answers accurately by describing the proposal one is adopting and carrying out. Acts, in their human reality as creations and expressions of one's reality as a person, are identified by or *specified by their objects.*[24]

That famous phrase is used by Aquinas interchangeably with another, equivalent phrase: *acts are specified by their intention(s).*[25] For, although Aquinas often distinguished between "intention" in the sense of one's ultimate or remote objective and "choice" in the sense of one's proximate objective, that is, one's chosen means (as in his commentary on Peter Lombard: III.2), he also often abandoned that distinction as irrelevant when he was considering the precise boundaries between right and wrong. For, to repeat: the object, the proposal adopted by choice, includes the end and the means alike; "intending" an end and willing the means are, he says, a single act of will, and moral reflection and analysis considers that whole act of will.[26]

In this perspective, *merely* behavioral differences fall away as morally irrelevant to identifying the type of wrong involved. For example: the behavioral difference between so-called actions (or positive actions) and omissions is morally irrelevant where each is chosen as a means. If we decide to kill our child or our aged aunt to collect on the insurance or the will, we may then settle on doing it with a pillow or a needle, or on achieving the same end simply by omitting to supply food. Either way, we have chosen an act of murder; bringing about death was built into the proposal, as the means we adopted in adopting that proposal by choice.

Conversely, states of affairs which are connected, perhaps even very closely and directly, with the carrying out and the

---

content of one's] willing [*ratio volendi*], the end and the means are one and the same object": *Summa Theologiae.* 1-2 q.12 a.4 ad 2.

24. *Summa Theol.* 1-2 q.18 aa.2c, 4c, 5c, 6c, 7c, 10c; *De malo* q.2 a.5 ad 9 ("finis proximus actus idem est quod objectum et ab hoc recipit [actus] speciem").

25. *Summa Theol.* 2-2 q.64 a.7c; equally, in effect, q.43 a.3c; 1-2 q.72 a.1c.

26. 1-2 q.12 a.4; q.19 a.2 ad 1.

outcome of one's action, but which are neither needed nor wanted as part of one's way of bringing about what one proposes to do and bring about, are unintended effects, *side effects*. Though they are caused by one's choice and action, they are not chosen, that is, are not intended, even if they are foreseen (even foreseen as certain). Rather, they are permitted, that is, (as I shall say), *accepted*. Certainly one has moral responsibility for what one thus knowingly and "deliberately" causes or brings about. But that responsibility is not the same as one's responsibility for what one chooses (intends) as part (whether as end or means) of one's proposal. Why is it not the same?

Every choice and action has some more or less immediate or remote negative impact—in some way tends to destroy, damage, or impede—some instantiation(s) of basic human goods. One can always refrain from the *choice to harm* an instance of a good. But one can never avoid *harming* some instances of human goods. Since it is inevitable that there will be some such harm, it cannot be excluded by reason's norms of action. For moral norms exclude irrationality, over which we have some control; they do not exclude accepting the inevitable limits we face as rational agents.

Thus, though one is responsible for the side effects of one's action, there can be no rational norm of the form, Do not cause harm, even as a side effect. But there is always a reason not to *intend* to harm human beings in any basic aspect of their good, and since (II.6) that reason cannot be outweighed by a weightier reason established prior to moral judgment and choice, there is no reason to override that first reason, which, therefore, is simply reason. In short, there is a principle of the form, Do not intend harm to a human being, either as an end or as a means. More precisely (and more precisely than Romans 3:8, though not outside its range): Do not do evil—destroy, damage, or impede a basic human good—that good may come.

The thus morally significant distinction between intention and acceptance of side effects is clear even when common speech obscures it. A woman who chooses to have her womb removed out of hatred of human procreation or as a means (perhaps reluctantly adopted) to enjoying sex without fear of pregnancy which would prevent the acquisition of a holiday house makes a different choice, performs a different act, from the woman who chooses to have it removed to avert the spread of a cancer. The acts are different, even though the behavior is identical; even though in common speech she could be said in each case to "be being sterilized," or even to be "getting herself sterilized," only the first two choices were choices *of sterilization*. Common speech, which is not systematically oriented toward precise moral understanding and is impressed by behavioral and consequential similarities and by legal categories, is not a safe guide. It uses all the action-related terms, including even *act* and *intention*, with an ambiguity which can be overcome only by careful attention to the importance of the end and means united in a proposal shaped by intelligent deliberation (however rapid) and adopted by choice.

The significance of the distinction between choosing (intending) ends or means and accepting side effects can be further clarified by considering directly the significance of choice. The form of "voluntariness" involved in knowingly causing side effects may well be culpable. But it cannot have the same self-constituting effect as the form of voluntariness we call intending (choosing). For choosing is adopting a proposal, and what one thus adopts is, so to speak, synthesized with one's will, that is, with oneself as an acting subject. One *becomes* what, seeing reason to, one chose: what one intended.

Forming an intention, in choosing freely, is not a matter of having an internal feeling or impression. Nor is it a matter of following a desire, in the sense of a feeling; even if quite reluctant, it will be self-constitutive, since intelligence and will are more constitutive of personal life than are feelings or emotions. Forming an intention is a matter of setting oneself to do something. Thus, for example, if one fails to do what one set oneself to do, *one has failed*. But if the foreseen side effects fail to materialize, one has in no way failed—indeed, if one adopted means with an eye to minimizing bad side effects, the nonoccurrence of those side effects enhances the worth and success of one's attempt.

And every choice, once made, lasts in one's character. As behavior, performance, cause, one's choice and action may be frustrated and utterly fail. But unless and until one repents of it—that is, reverses it by some contrary, incompatible choice—one retains the character which one specified and created for oneself by intelligently shaping and freely adopting the object of that choice, the proposal one synthesized with one's will by choice. The lastingness, the persistence, of choice is something which the tradition of philosophical and theological reflection did not make sufficiently explicit until recently.[27] It is very important for an understanding of the relation between this-worldly actions and the completed Kingdom in heaven, and of the sacramental continuation of Christ's salvific acts, and, as I am now indicating, of every morally significant choice's self-constitutive significance. Thus it is important to understanding the significance of moral norms, particularly specific moral absolutes, which specify acts by their shaping intention rather than by reference to their side effects (even in the case of those norms, particularly concerning sex, where built-in side effects are intrinsically related to the wrongness of a type of act).

To summarize: The *intention* of an act has the significance it has in the identification and evaluation of the act, precisely because *choice* has the creative self-constitutive importance it has. That importance is so great that Aquinas placed the whole

27. See now Germain Grisez, *The Way of the Lord Jesus*, vol. 1 *Christian Moral Principles* (Chicago: Franciscan Herald Press, 1983) 52, 70; Karol Wojtyla, *The Acting Person* (Dordrecht, Boston, London: Reidel, 1979) 13, 19, 149–52, 160, on the "persistent" "intransitive" effects of chosen action; Finnis, *Fundamentals of Ethics* 139–44, 153. The idea is certainly present in the tradition, in the idea that sinners need a new heart, in the theological ideas of mortal sin and the stain of sin, and in notions about virtues and vices. What these elements in the tradition fail to articulate is the constitutive and dynamic aspect of the lastingness of choice. Grisez analogizes this to intellectual knowledge, which lasts by constituting a dynamic framework, making one capable of and disposed to further knowledge.

of his mature work on ethics under this prologue: "Since man is said to be made in the image of God because 'image' here refers to intelligent and free choice. . . , let us consider man, that image, precisely insofar as he is himself the origin of his own deeds, through having free choice and power over those deeds." [28]

4. Intending human harm: never acceptable for God or man

But perhaps our human status as images of God tells against my argument? For if human persons are in the image of God, and if God can intend evils for the sake of the good of the universe, why should not we, too, intend evils as means to greater good? Perhaps Romans 3:5–8 has a message other than we discerned; perhaps it means that God can do whatever redounds to his greater glory, even if Paul and the rest of us are subject to some scarcely intelligible law against emulating our creator?

As Paul would say: By no means! Christian thought has insisted that God does not intend evils, not even as means, and that he only permits them, as a side effect of what he does intend for the sake of the good of the whole universe (the expression of his own goodness, his glory).

The distinction between intention (including of means) and permission (that is, accepting the foreseen side effects of one's own choices) is employed definitively by the Council of Trent, in one of its canons on justification, in the course of defending the reality of free choice: "If anyone says that it is not in man's power to make his ways evil, but that God performs the evil works just as he performs the good, not only permissively but also properly and *per se*. . . : *anathema sit*." [29] What does *per se* mean here? There can be no doubt about its meaning in the terminology stabilized for the scholastic theological tradition by

28. *Summa Theol.* 1-2 prol. and q.1 a.1c.
29. Sess. 6 [1547 A.D.], can. 6; *Denz.-Schoen.* 1556.

Aquinas, on the basis of Aristotle's *Physics* 8,4. Aquinas explains it thus: In relation to purposeful actions [*propter finem*], "something is spoken of as *per se* when it is intended [*intentum*], and is said to be *per accidens* when it is outside the intention [*praeter intentionem*]."[30] Or again: "In moral matters . . . , what is intended is *per se*, whereas what follows *praeter intentionem* may be regarded as *per accidens*."[31] There are many passages in which Aquinas draws this same distinction between the *per se* and the *per accidens*, and in which the linking idea is the distinction between what is intended and what, for one reason or another, lies outside the agent's intention.[32] And of these numerous passages, many make it clear that, in these contexts, "intention" extends not only to ultimate ends but also to proximate means.[33]

Trent's similar use of *per se* manifestly means the same thing. Neither as end nor as means does God in any way intend human evil (the canon gives an instance: Judas' treachery); God merely permits it.

The defined dogma of faith pertains to God's permission of human sin; a foreseen and permitted side effect of his creation of human free choice. And some proportionalists, following Schüller, wish to draw a sharp distinction: God's holiness (they oddly call it his "moral will" as distinct from his "creative will") is incompatible with his in any way intending human sin; but God, and therefore also human persons, can rightly intend premoral evils.[34] We need not recall here the unanswered difficulty

---

30. *Summa Theol.* 2-2 q.59 a.2c. "[something is done] *per accidens* insofar as it happens *praeter intentionem operantis.* . . . For we are said to do *per se* and not *per accidens* those things which we intend to do. Nothing is specified in terms of what is *per accidens*; things are specified only by what is *per se* . . .": *In eth.* 5 lect. 13, nn. 1035–36; see similarly 7 lect. 9 n. 1438.

31. 2-2 q.39 a.1c.

32. And Aquinas sometimes links *directe et per se*, as opposed to *indirecte vel per accidens*, the distinction being precisely that in the former case what is willed *directe et per se* is willed as a means: 1-2 q.76 a.4.

33. E.g. 1-2 q.76 a.4c; 2-2 q.37 a.1c; q.39 a.1c; q.43 a.3c; q.64 a.7c. See likewise Cajetan on the last-cited text.

34. Thus James J. Walter, "Response to John Finnis: A Theological Critique," in Thomas G. Fuechtmann, ed., *Consistent Ethic of Life* (Kansas City:

(II.4) which Schüller and others face in explaining why, on proportionalist principles, one may not rightly intend the sin of another as a means to reducing the overall number or gravity of sins. More significant here is a related question. Why should the difference between intending and permitting be relevant, as Schüller admits, in relation to one's involvement in the wrongdoing of other people, but irrelevant, as he insists, in relation to one's involvement in any and every other kind of evil? But what is *most* significant here is this: The proportionalist willingness to intend premoral human evil (the destruction or damaging or impeding of human persons in basic aspects of their reality and fulfillment)[35] jars against the massive tradition of theological reflection on the divine will and providence, expounded by Aquinas and before him by St. John Damascene, the last of the Fathers (c. 745 A.D.). For that tradition insists, vigorously, that for God to will *per se* (that is, intend) *anything* which intelligence would call an evil is inconsistent with his holiness.[36]

Sheed & Ward, 1988) 186–87, thinks that Aquinas in *Summa Theol.* 1-2 q.19 a.9 accepts that God wills the evil of natural defects for the sake of the preservation of the natural order; Walter then exclaims that neither he himself "nor any other proportionalist can see here how God's moral will is only disposed indirectly or permissively vis-à-vis non-moral evil (natural defect)." Walter misreads a.9 by ignoring the ad 3m, which establishes that God does not will evils to be, and that the only sense in which he wills even natural defects is that he wills to permit them. Walter also thinks, mistakenly, that *per se* means, in effect, *propter se* (as an end in itself), and is thus contrasted with *propter aliud* (i.e., with "as a means"); in fact, however, the everywhere more usual and here certainly the relevant contrast is with *per accidens*, and that contrast is precisely between the intended and the "outside intention."

35. Some proportionalists, notably Josef Fuchs, are unwilling to admit that they countenance intending such harm and speak instead of causing, occasioning, provoking, allowing, "*indirectly* intending," and so on. But analysis of the acts which they countenance but the tradition excluded as *intrinsece mala* shows that, even for these authors (as for other, less squeamish proportionalists), the difference between intending a result and causing a result plays no real part in *reaching* their judgment on the morality of acts.

36. See John of Damascus, *De fide orthodoxa* 2, 29; Aquinas, *Summa Theol.* 1 q.19 a.9; Patrick Lee, "Permanence of the Ten Commandments: St. Thomas and His Modern Commentators," *Theolological Studies* 42 (1981) 422 at 435–36. The thought is compactly expressed, without the differentiation, in Hippolytus around 225 A.D. in his *Philosophumena*, book 10,33; the differentiation between results of which God as creator is "altogether the cause" and results of which, though foreseeing them, he is "not altogether the cause," is made in the same decade in Origen's *Commentary on Genesis* book 3,6; the distinction of

Christian reflection on God and his holy will, and Christian reflection on the morality of human choosing and doing, thus develop together in mutual support. Together they mark a large advance in differentiated understanding over pre-Christian philosophy and philosophical theology. Philo Judaeus, Christ's contemporary, will insist (like Plato) that God is not the cause of evils and is not responsible for them; but Philo's explanations derail into a strange theory of agency in which the principal is not answerable for the acts of his agents; corruption and destruction are brought about not by God but "by certain others as ministers [of the sovereign King]."[37] Christian reflection advances decisively beyond the undifferentiated concept of "cause," replacing it with the act-analytical distinctions between choosing or intending and permitting or accepting. As one reads through the writings of sophisticated proportionalist moralists of the late twentieth century, one sees with amazement that they everywhere lose their grip on the distinction. They have fallen back into the undifferentiated problematic of "causing" evils (including, of course, the Enlightenment extension of "cause" to include whatever one could have prevented but did not, a concept incompatible with Christian understanding of divine holiness).[38]

_____

permissive from intending will emerges in Augustine and is clearly stated by Fulgentius around 520 in his *Ad monimum* 1,13. Especially illuminating is Aquinas *De veritate* q.5 a.4, obj.10 and ad 10, arguing that doing evil/causing harm (*facere malum*) is wholly foreign to good persons, whether human or divine, but that "ordering" evil/harm, by permitting it on account of some good that can thereby ensue, is consistent with divine goodness. In a.4c he stresses that natural defects (e.g., congenital deformities) are "means" only in the sense that God turns them to good effect; they are not "means" in the sense that every intended means is (viz. not only a means but also an [intermediate] end).

37. Philo, *Questions and Answers on Genesis* 1, q.23; see also qq. 68, 78, 89, 100; 2, q.13; *De confusione linguarum*, c.36, para. 180.

38. See, e.g., Bruno Schüller, S.J., "La moralité des moyens," *Recherches de Science Religieuse* 68 (1980) 205 at 211 (*causing* moral evil is never justified, *causing* nonmoral evils is justified in pursuit of nonmoral good of corresponding importance), 221–22 ("pour tous les biens dont la possession contribue au bien-être de l'homme . . . [q]uoi que l'on choisisse . . . les conséquences négatives qui résultent du choix sont un pur moyen en vue des conséquences positives qui en résultent"); Peschke, "Tragfähigkeit und Grenzen des Prinzips der Doppelwirkung," *Studia Moralia* 26 (1988) 101 at 110–12, where Peschke states the "principle of double effect" (which he ascribes to Catholic theology and attacks) in terms not of what is directly or indirectly willed or intended or chosen or done

5. Counterexamples

Still, can it really be true that one may never rightly intend human harm even as a means to human good? Garth Hallett, S.J., intends a decisive one-sentence argument against the whole traditional distinction between intention and side effect when he insists: "Love not only permits but repeatedly requires non-morally evil means: disagreeable medicine, distressing criticism, painful punishment, fatiguing labor, and so forth."[39] The criticism simply overlooks the distinction it claims to criticize. The fatigue induced by labor, the bitterness of medicine, the distress occasioned by honest criticism—all are side effects, not means.

Richard McCormick, S.J., makes a more careful attempt to show that the tradition was inconsistent with any principle of the form, Do not intentionally harm human good. Do not do evil for the sake of good. His list of intended harms allowed in the tradition encompasses (i) intended deception of another when necessary for the protection of, for example, the confessional secret; (ii) intended amputation of a leg to prevent spread of cancer; (iii) intended death of the criminal in capital punishment; (iv) intended death of assailant in cases of self-defense; (v) intended pain of the child whom we spank pedagogically.[40]

Item (iv) should be removed immediately. As McCormick half concedes, Aquinas denies that one who is defending himself may rightly intend the death of his assailant, even as a means of self-defense, though one may, if necessary, adopt means of self-defense which one knows will cause death as an unintended side effect.[41] Quite a few in the tradition have disagreed, but many have agreed, as I do. Item (i) should equally be removed; the

---

but in terms of what is directly/indirectly "caused"; Josef Fuchs, *Christian Ethics in a Secular Arena* (Washington, D.C.: Georgetown University Press; Dublin: Gill & Macmillan, 1984) 85 ("prohibitive moral norms which forbid an act because it causes a pre-moral wrong . . .").

39. *Christian Moral Reasoning* 112.
40. McCormick, *Notes . . . 1965 through 1980*, 647. Franz Scholz treats as decisive the pain a mother causes her child when she puts disinfectant on his wound: see ibid., 808.
41. *Summa Theol.* 2-2 q.64 a.7.

tradition does not judge that one may rightly lie to protect a confessional secret, nor that one may intend more than that inquirers with no right to the truth should remain in their ignorance. Then item (ii) should go; therapeutic amputation is not doing harm but preventing the further harm that a limb already doomed would do to the health or life of the person. Moreover, the basic goods to be respected in every choice are aspects of the fulfillment not of this or that organ but of the whole human individual; that individual's bodily health is integral, not merely instrumental, to that fulfillment, but it is measured as the good of an organic whole. So the transplantation of a duplicated organ such as the kidney, leaving the whole substantially unimpaired, need not be regarded as doing harm for the sake of good.

Then item (v) should fall away, too. Pain is not itself an intelligible evil; indeed, it is itself an intelligible good, as one can understand by considering the difficult, usually short lives of those born with no sense of pain. Pain is experienced as a sensory evil; the horror it arouses in us is essential to its intelligible function. But it is an intelligible human evil only insofar as it causes disturbance to the inner harmony of one's feelings with each other and with reason, and to all the other harmonies dependent on inner harmony. Spanking a child (and Hallett's "painful punishment"), when rightly done, is done precisely to restore that harmony and the interpersonal harmonies dependent on it. It need involve no harm to health or life, no intelligible evil at all, and therefore no intention to do harm for the sake of good.

There remains, then, item (iii): capital punishment. It will be helpful first to reflect on the concept of punishment. Insofar as it is intended only to be preventive or reformative, punishment can be chosen without including in its precise object any negative impact whatsoever on any good; the negative impact on various goods valued by offenders can be accepted as a side effect of benefits sought for them and for society. Insofar as it is chosen precisely for the sake of deterring others, the justifiability of punishment is, to say the least, entirely questionable. But there need be nothing wrong in welcoming the deterrent side effects of punishment otherwise justified. The justification of punishment, as a practice distinguishable from preventative or reformative control of the insane or infectious, must always be retributive. Punishment is not revenge. It is the restoration of a balance of fairness which the offender's crime, being essentially a willful choice to prefer his own freedom of action to the rights of others, has necessarily disturbed. Restoring that balance requires that offenders undergo something contrary to their will, just as they voluntarily imposed on others what was contrary to *their* will.[42]

However, punishment does not require more than that offenders be deprived of something they value or desire, such as instrumental goods like property or liberty, or sensory satisfactions which are not inseparably connected to basic human goods. The principle which excludes choosing to destroy, damage, or impede basic goods does not forbid a retributive penalty focused on instrumental and sensory goods, as a means to blocking not the realization of any basic human good, but only some of the desires and some aspects of the willing of the one punished.

But does not the infliction of capital punishment entail a choice to destroy a basic human good, human bodily life itself? Here there is room, it seems to me, for debate and further reflection, such as that on which the church itself, I think, is engaged. It seems possible to hold that, just insofar as the action chosen immediately and of itself instantiates the good of retributive justice, the death of the one punished is not being chosen either as an end in itself or as a means to an ulterior end. Others disagree. All, however, should agree that the truth of the great principle that evil may not be done for the sake of good cannot be made to turn on its conformity to some prior judgment (such as the church has never definitively made) that capi-

42. See John Finnis, *Natural Law and Natural Rights* (Oxford and New York: Oxford University Press, 1980) 262–64.

tal punishment is a justifiable exercise of the right and responsibility of rulers to punish, a right which the church certainly has
proposed as a truth to be held definitively.

6. Responsibility for side effects: other principles and norms

How, then, should one regard the consequences which one
foresees one will or may well bring about, and which one in that
sense "chooses to cause" though does not intend, that is, does
not choose (whether as end or as means)? What is one's moral
responsibility for these?

Often great. But it is not measured by the principle that evil
may not be chosen, whether for the sake of injury (revenge) or of
good. Therefore, one's responsibility for consequences is not
measured by the specific absolute moral norms which express
that principle's implications in relation to particular basic human goods. Instead it is measured by the principle of fairness
(the Golden Rule), and by all the other basic moral principles.
(These further principles, which I have not here explored, call for
creativity and fidelity in making and carrying out commitments,
a certain detachment from particular goals, and all the other
virtues needed to bring feelings and actions into harmony with
reason's grasp of the basic human goods.)[43]

Fairness is an objective measure, requiring rational impar-
tiality as between persons. It imposes reason's sway over all the
feelings which deflect one toward a partiality not rooted in the
intelligible requirements, in this finite world, of the basic human
goods themselves. But though it is a rational and objective
standard of judgment, fairness's implications, and the standard's
applications, depend on feelings which others may not share and
commitments which others may not have made.

Indeed, to apply the Golden Rule, to make sense of "as you
would have others do to you," one must be able to commensu-

---

43. Ibid., chap. 5; also see Grisez, *Christian Moral Principles*, chap. 8.

rate burdens and benefits as they affect oneself, in order to know what one considers *too great an evil* to accept. One carries out this commensuration by reference to factors more or less peculiar to oneself, particularly one's prior commitments and one's intuitive awareness ("discernment") of one's own differentiated feelings toward various goods and bads as concretely remembered, experienced, or imagined. (This is not, of course, the sort of commensuration proportionalists need, for their claim is to employ a rational and objective premoral commensuration, and one which could override [other] moral principles and norms.) The feelings of good persons are, for the most part, integrated with their prior commitments, their sense of vocation. That one adopt some such vocational commitments is certainly a requirement of reason, but reason rarely if ever directs the choice of vocation toward a single, rationally determined option.

Analogously, in the life of a community, the preliminary commensuration of rationally incommensurable factors is accomplished not by rationally determined judgments but by *decisions*.

 Thus all the institutions and practices shaped and regulated by the principle of fairness are more or less relative to times and places—unlike the moral absolutes (including, of course, the *principle* of fairness itself). Is it fair to drive at a speed which can kill? In our society it is. For, by the fair procedures of custom and legislation, we have chosen to accept for ourselves these risks, imposing like risks on others, as a side effect of goods we esteem. But if a society chose by fair procedures to restrict vehicles to walking pace, we could scarcely criticize the fairness of the decision, just as members of that society could not criticize the fairness of ours. The good and bad consequences of such decisions, and of such ways of life, are truly not commensurable by reason. Here, as in countless lesser decisions, only the feelings of the prudent provide the measure.

But the "prudent," whose feelings are the right measure, are not the worldly wise, or the cautious and risk averse, but the *phronimoi* or *spoudaioi*, the *prudentes*, mature people of practical wisdom. Part of their prudence, their justice, their love of neighbor as themselves, their seeking the Kingdom first, is precisely their firm integration of character around *all* the moral absolutes, their unwillingness even to deliberate about departing from one or other of them.

CHAPTER IV

Challenge and Response

1. Contraception and the general denial of absolutes

How, then, did so many Catholic moralists come to reject *and formally attack and denounce* the church's constant and firm teaching of specific moral absolutes? And to embrace *and teach* theories which in secular philosophical debates had long ago proved incapable of withstanding rational criticism?

Secular thinkers, of course, had generally rejected the absolutes. Their understanding that reason does not support the moral alternatives did not deflect their will to adopt principles of action which promised to preserve social peace, prosperity, and liberty of action within whatever community and era formed the horizon of their practical interest. So it would be easy to conclude that Catholic moralists, and the bishops, priests, religious, and laity who followed them, simply fell in with the unbelieving common notions of their age, losing coherent faith in God's providence and plan for constituting in this world a people with horizons and destiny no narrower than integral human fulfillment itself.

Nor would that conclusion be mistaken. Secularism has indeed affected the thought and practice of many Christians. To everything in this chapter about the specific reasons for dissent from the church's moral teaching, one should add the influence of contemporaneous dissent in other areas of faith and theology: denials of the bodily resurrection of Jesus, of his exclusive mediatorship, of anything like defined doctrine on original sin, of the bodily presence of Jesus in the Eucharist, of Mary's perpetual virginity, and so forth. Dissent in one area has reinforced dissent in others, in both directions.[1]

Still, the conclusion that dissent in moral theology is simply a surrender to secularism remains too simple. More can be said— much more, of course, than I can say here, or than anyone, I imagine, fully sees and understands.

One fact seems clear and basic. The formal attack on the moral absolutes emerges, among Catholics, in response to the problem of contraception. Not in response to the desire to maintain a counterpopulation deterrent strategy of annihilating retaliation; or to tell lies in military, police, and political operations; or to carry out therapeutic abortions; or to arrange homosexual unions; or to relieve inner tensions and disequilibria by masturbation; or to keep slaves; or to produce babies by impersonal artifice. Those desires were and are all urgent enough, but none of them precipitated the formal rejection of moral absolutes. The desire to practice or to approve contraception did.

The old canon law embodied an understanding of contraception more accurate than neoscholastic theology's. To contracept, one must think that some behavior is likely to cause a new human life to begin, and that such a beginning of a new life could be impeded by some other behavior one could perform, and one chooses to perform the latter with the intention that that prospective new life not begin. That choice is entirely distinct from the choice to engage in the behavior which might cause life to begin. The contraceptive choice is related to sexual acts only instrumentally, insofar as it lessens the likelihood of pregnancy and thus removes or weakens a motive for avoiding intercourse. Being thus a distinct chosen act, contraception is defined by its

---

1. For an indication of some intrinsic connections between these matters of dissent, see John C. Ford, Germain Grisez, Joseph Boyle, John Finnis, and William E. May, *The Teaching of Humanae Vitae: A Defense* (San Francisco: Ignatius Press, 1988) 107–8. For a general account of how things went bad in the church, see Grisez, "How to Deal with Theological Dissent" in Charles Curran and Richard McCormick, S.J., *Dissent in Moral Theology* (New York: Paulist Press, 1988).

intention, which simply is that a prospective new human life not begin. Choosing to contracept is simply contralife, whatever else may then be said, and rightly said, about the morally significant features of the sexual act performed *as* contracepted. Thus, the church's universal canon law, from its inception until 1917 (and thus too those Fathers whose thought was crystallized in this canon), identified contraception as an act wrongful precisely because, as a choice, contralife.[2]

Many factors affected and still affect people's grasp of this specifying characteristic of contraception. Theologians often assessed contraception's morality exclusively in terms of the character of the contracepted sexual act, not a surprising tendency at times when the standard model of contraception was withdrawal (onanism). Another factor was, and is, that periodic abstinence can certainly be chosen precisely as a means of carrying out the contralife choice to impede the coming-to-be of a new child. "Natural Family Planning" (NFP) can certainly be adopted as one method of contraception.[3] (But it need not be adopted with that intention. The system of identifying fertile times and avoiding intercourse at those times can, instead, be followed by couples who form no *intention to impede* the coming-to-be of a new child, and who in following that system of avoiding intercourse intend only to avoid the bad side effects which having a baby would bring about. In *their* practice of NFP there is no *choice* whose meaning is: to prevent a possible baby's coming-to-be.)

Our cultural environment is now shaped by the assumption that regular sexual satisfaction is a natural right and a kind of obligation for a married couple. It is an environment just as indifferent to fine but fundamental differences in the way human

2. See Ford, et al., *Teaching of Humanae Vitae* 36–37, quoting the canon *Si aliquis* of Gregory IX, on the antecedents and adoption of which see also John T. Noonan, *Contraception* (New York: Mentor Books, 1965) 122 (St. Hippolytus, circa 225) 127–28 (St. John Chrysostom, circa 391) 128–29 (St. Ambrose, circa 390) 129–30, (St. Jerome, circa 384) 208–10, 217–19

3. See Ford, et al., *Teaching of Humanae Vitae* 81–82 (and the citation to John Paul II on 81).

will relates to human good as to the distinction between God's willing good and his permitting evil. In such an environment, the pastoral care of Catholics became very difficult.

The pastoral problems were exacerbated by the notably weak and ambiguous form in which the moral theology of recent centuries articulated the intrinsic connections between the service of human goods through free choices and the building up of the Kingdom (compare I.3). In relation to contraception, that theology usually proposed, as primary, an argument (about not perverting faculties) which left the specific relation between contraception and any basic human good quite unclear. In popular preaching, that argument, in turn, led to an attempt to explain the wrongness of contraception by reference to the morally irrelevant distinction between the natural and the *artificial*. But, more generally, the standard theology tended to propose not truths about the intrinsic relationship of certain types of act to true integral human fulfillment but a series of laws. And with the idea of law came the usual conceptual concomitants of human laws: ignorance excuses; dispensations are conceivable; obedience is to the formulated rule not the underlying rationale, but the formulated rule is subject to *"epikeia,"* and penalties, having no intrinsic relation to the objective wrongfulness of an act, so can be withheld or imposed in pursuit of other purposes.

One particular manifestation of this legalism was a pastoral practice called "leaving people in good faith." Such a practice, although it doubtless has a place, runs into grave difficulties when sought to be applied to a practical principle as evident as that human life is to be respected, and to options as clearly opposed to that principle as acts whose exclusive intention is to impede the coming-to-be of a human life. For a long time, this practice could be given some anchorage in the realities of choice by the assumption or presumption that particular contraceptive choices were "sins of weakness," made under the swamping influence of immediate sexual passion. Always vulnerable to questions, this presumption became unsustainable with the advent of the pill. For the choice to take the pill, and keep on taking it day after day, lacks even the appearance of a will overwhelmed by passion.[4]

Moreover, the failure to identify clearly and centrally the most relevant moral absolute violated by contraception meant that NFP was commonly taught and practiced without distinguishing between a technique for effecting a contralife intention to prevent the coming-to-be of a baby and a technique for calculating when one might have intercourse both without irresponsibly courting the bad effects of having another baby *and* without choosing to prevent those bad effects by preventing the coming-to-be of a baby. Again, the Christian moral truth that conjugal intercourse has a unitive significance—not a new truth, but just then being enthusiastically articulated in fresh ways—was not carefully distinguished from the secular claim that sexual release and expression by orgasm are simply necessary for personal well-being, if not universally then at least within a relationship such as marriage.

For these reasons, at least, the pastoral pressure became most intense just at a time of general ferment in the church (and Western society). And there emerged, unmistakably, a settled will to make whatever transformations of the teaching on contraception might be necessary to relieve that pressure.

Thus there emerged first the notion that the pill, leaving the behavioral aspects of sexual intercourse untouched, lacked the moral character of contraception. This feeble theory, developed by Louis Janssens, who was to become one of the three principal

4. Against a suggestion that pastoral practice should "have recourse to the diminution of the subjective responsibility of many married people," those theologians on Paul VI's Commission for the Study of Problems of Family, Population and Birth who had opted for a change in the church's teaching quite reasonably objected: faithful Catholics experiencing difficulties in this matter are (they noted) more and more repelled by this "interpretation" of a decision which they make knowing full well that it involves their personal responsibility; to such couples it seems incoherent to teach a very rigorous precept and then to cast about for means of "not having to urge its rigor," or for confessors to remain silent about it when confronted by couples who face the exigencies of their married life with full lucidity. "Rapport Final" of 27 June 1966 (unpublished).

architects of proportionalist moral theology,[5] could not and did not survive a year's discussion. It was transformed into the theory we find in the documents of 1966 in Paul VI's commission. The contraceptive act and the contracepted sexual act constitute only one act, whose moral character is derived entirely from the moral character of the sexual act. This in turn attains its essential moral character from the "totality" constituted of itself, the series of contracepted acts of which it forms a part, and the non-contracepted sexual acts which there have been or may be in the course of a married lifetime.[6] This theory, too—on which the church was meant to have reversed its teaching of contraception and promulgated a new teaching that contraception is often morally obligatory—could not withstand a touch of rational reflection and has rightly disappeared without trace.[7]

But the will to justify contraception for Catholics did not weaken. Hence there emerged a series of arguments seeking to reshape the very foundations of Catholic moral theology, so that those foundations might cease to provide obstacles to accepting the conclusion desired.

And these arguments have had their effect. Today virtually no Catholic theologian who dissents on contraception dissents only on contraception. Virtually all who dissent on contracep-

---

5. "Morale conjugale et progestogènes" *Ephemerides Theologicae Lovaniensis* 39 (1963) 787–826; for a summary, see Ambrogio Valsecchi, *Controversy: The Birth Control Debate 1958–1968* (London: Geoffrey Chapman, 1968) 38–40 (the book conveniently summarizes the debate from 1962 to 1967). For an analysis of the debate among Catholic theologians, see John Finnis, "*Humanae Vitae*: Its Background and Aftermath" *International Review of National Family Planning* 4 (1980) 141-53. On Janssens's later, proportionalist general theory, see William E. May, "Aquinas and Janssens on the Moral Meaning of Human Acts," *The Thomist* 48 (1984) 566–606.

6. Working Paper of 27 May 1966, translated in Peter Harris, ed., *On Human Life* (London: Burns & Oates, 1968) at 211–12 (the section is headed "Intervention [i.e., contraception] is well explained within the limits of the classic doctrine"!); see also pt. 2.2 of the commission's report, translated at 232. The argument is articulated by Paul VI in para. 3 and formally rejected in para. 14 of *Humanae Vitae*.

7. Or rather, it collapsed into the general proportionalist theory that the morality of a choice can be assessed only by taking into account *all* the circumstances, a totality far wider, of course, than the supposed "totality" constituted by the couple's imagined series of marital acts past, present, and future.

tion deny that there can be any exceptionless norms of the sort that *all* teachers of the Catholic faith publicly upheld down to about 1965.[8]

2. Historical and ecclesiological skirmishes

Remarkably persistent have been the attempts to gain authoritative support for proportionalism by reading back into the high scholasticism of Bonaventure, Albert, and Thomas the essential proportionalist positions: acts have their moral character from their end, and an end is a state of affairs, attainable by human action, which makes the action right because rationally judged to promise the greater overall net premoral good or lesser overall net premoral evil. How far the high scholastics in fact were from accepting the views ascribed to them by Scholz, Dedek, Janssens and McCormick has been shown earlier.[9] I need only add one or two points.

Much play is made with Aquinas's statement that derived moral norms, since they involve contingent particulars, hold not universally but only generally (*ut in pluribus*), subject to exceptions (*ut in paucioribus*).[10] This is made a primary support for the claim that, for Aquinas, the rules which late scholasticism supposed to be exceptionless are only generalizations, rules of thumb. In truth, however, the relevant generalization is not the

8. On this fact, and on the corresponding shift of opinion among the Catholic laity, see Ford, et al., *Teaching of Humanae Vitae* 21–22. Francis Hürth, "Instructio Supremae Sacrae Congregationis S. Officii de Ethica Situationis," *Periodica de re Morali Canonica Liturgica* 45 (1956) 137 at 185–91, makes it clear that for more than twenty-five years before 1956 there were some theologians who, in their intramural teaching, upheld the view that certain acts which in ordinary situations are intrinsically wrong become perceptible to conscience, in extraordinary situations or conflicts, as right. The examples reported by Hürth are (in his order) contraception, direct abortion, masturbation, suicide.

9. William E. May's study of Janssens's interpretation of Aquinas, "Aquinas and Janssens," *The Thomist* 48 (1984) 566, demonstrates the scale and boldness of the misreadings involved.

10. *Summa Theologiae*. 1-2 q.94 a.4c. Proportionalists who appeal to this text omit to note that the question under discussion in a.4 has nothing to do with the question whether there are any exceptionless moral norms. It is, Is the natural law the same for all?, and none of the counterpositions which Aquinas articulates in order to refute has any relation to the moral absolutes of the tradition.

tradition's moral absolutes but this statement of Aquinas. That moral norms are generalizations and are subject to exceptions is only a generalization; it is subject to exception. This is made clear many times by Aquinas, when he notes that, although affirmative moral norms, the majority of moral norms, hold *semper sed non ad semper*, there are also negative moral norms, the minority, which hold *semper et ad semper*, always and everywhere without exceptions. His very illustration of the way general norms are subject to exception makes this plain enough; the norm that what you have borrowed you should return states an affirmative responsibility and so is subject to exceptions: if the lender has turned into a traitor or a madman, and what you borrowed is a weapon—occurrences which are exceptional—then the norm, being based on principles of fairness and reciprocity, does not require them to be returned then and there.[11]

Then again, some play is made with Aquinas's treatment of divine dispensations. The main proportionalist discussions, by Milhaven and Dedek, have been analyzed and dismantled in a study by Patrick Lee which repays reading and rereading.[12] Suffice it to note that whenever Thomas formally considers the question in its own right, he consistently gives and defends the answer: No, God cannot dispense from the Decalogue's commands; to do so would be inconsistent with his wisdom.[13] Whenever he speaks of dispensations from precepts of the Decalogue, he is using the notion of dispensation in a loose sense, relative to a loose understanding of the precept in which it is understood as forbidding acts specified, not by the precise object of the will, but rather by their physical characteristics as such, or according to some *conventional* (not critical) categorization.[14]

11. 1-2 q.94 a.4c.

12. "Permanence of the Ten Commandments: St. Thomas and His Modern Commentators," *Theological Studies* 42 (1981) 422.

13. 3 *Sent.* d.37 q.un. a.4c and ad 1; *Summa Theol.* 1-2 q.100 a.8; see also q.94 a.5 ad 2.

14. *Sent.* 1 d. 47, q. 1 a.4; 4 d.33, q.1, a.2; *De malo*, q.3 a.1 ad 17. It is worth remarking that, today, a theological reflection on the scriptural passages describing conduct which Aquinas felt bound to reconcile with divine law would be slower to assume that those passages *assert* the rightness of the conduct in question. Only those propositions asserted by the sacred writers of Scripture are

Finally one may mention, as a curiosity of the late sixties, Milhaven's suggestion that modern people, by virtue of their modernity of spirit (humankind come of age), may have a sort of standing dispensation from God to pursue what appears to them the greater premoral good or lesser premoral evil.[15] Fancies such as that passed muster more readily in 1968 than now, though the hubristic assumption of spiritual progress on which they are based has not fully dissipated.

A more popular fancy of the eighties is that modern moral problems are so *complex* that no revealed norm could truly settle them. The church's authority to teach *de moribus* is therefore limited to inspiring or admonitory generalizations. Some play is made with passages in which the council states, soberly enough, that the church does not have an immediate answer to every moral problem.[16] The question that occurs to the observer is, How long can these theologians keep on overlooking the distinction, not very abstruse, between "some" and "all," or between "not every" and "not any," so that they can continue to slide from "The church cannot give a specific answer to *every* moral question" to "The church cannot teach with definitive authority *any* specific moral norm"?[17] Glissading non sequiturs

asserted by the Holy Spirit and therefore certainly true; and not everything said or stated is, given its literary genre, the asserting of a proposition: cf. Vatican II, *Dei Verbum* 11.

15. John Giles Milhaven, "Moral Absolutes in Thomas Aquinas," in Charles Curran, ed., *Absolutes in Moral Theology* (Washington, D.C.: Corpus Books, 1968) 154–85; also in John Giles Milhaven, *Toward a New Catholic Morality* (New York: Doubleday, 1972) 136–67, 228–36. See also Franz Scholz, "Problems on Norms Raised by Ethical Borderline Situations: Beginnings of a Solution in Thomas Aquinas and Bonaventure," in Charles Curran and Richard McCormick, S.J., *Readings in Moral Theology No. 1: Moral Norms and Catholic Tradition* (New York: Paulist Press, 1979) 158 at 173, 178.

16. Especially *Gaudium et Spes* 33: "The Church, which guards the deposit of God's word, drawing from it principles of the religious and moral order, though she does not always have a ready answer to particular questions, desires to join the light of revelation with everyone's experience, so that the path mankind has recently taken may be illuminated." This is quoted, with intent to undercut the magisterial proclamation of specific moral absolutes, also in John Mahoney, *The Making of Moral Theology* (Oxford University Press, 1987) 303 (and cf. the statement by Fr. Mahoney and the vicar general of Westminster dated 30 June 1986, in *Briefing* 18 July 1986, 186–87.)

17. See, e.g. Francis A. Sullivan, S.J., *Magisterium* (Dublin: Gill & Macmillan,

which seem more at home in politics are to be found, remarkably, in serious theological books, and they serve for a time.[18]

3. The main action: in philosophical theology

Meanwhile, the main action, to which these skirmishes into history and ecclesiology were merely auxiliary, continued in the arena of philosophical theology. Theologians who had decided that to exclude contraception from married life is simply intolerable continued their struggle to find reasons which would show the reasonableness of that settled decision. With the rapid collapse and disappearance of the attempted revisions of classical moral theology (IV.1)—Janssens's behavior-focused revision to justify the pill, and Paul VI's commission's "total"-act revision to justify contraception—the campaign to develop a moral theory had to begin operating over a very wide front. It now went to the foundations. Contraception ceased to be the focus of theoretical consideration. The new objective became to show that the church's teaching that there are true specific moral

---

1984) 151. Non sequitur. A particularly vivid expression of the fallacious slide from "not all" to "not any" is Josef Fuchs, *Christian Ethics in a Secular Arena* (Washington, D.C.: Georgetown University Press; Dublin: Gill & Macmillan, 1984) 60, arguing that *no* matter of natural law could belong to the indirect or secondary object of infallibility, *because* "it does not seem conceivable that *the unlimited number* of concrete questions regarding the moral rightness of 'horizontal' acting have such a[n inner] relationship [to explicitly revealed truths] and therefore belong to the competence of the magisterium in the same full sense as revealed truths do" (emphasis added). Not all the many—therefore none.

18. See, e.g., Sullivan, *Magisterium* 150–51, where the argument is as follows: Modern moral problems are complex; therefore no specific moral requirements decisive for any modern moral problem are to be found within revelation. Non sequitur. Some modern moral problems are complex; some modern moral problems were moral problems two thousand years ago; some ancient moral problems which are still moral problems were complex then, as now. There are some manifestly revealed moral requirements manifestly relevant to some perennial moral problems, e.g., as to the dissolubility of true marriage. For another glissade from "not all" to "none," consider the argument by Gerard J. Hughes, S.J., that because revelation cannot override or supersede all our prior moral judgments, therefore revelation can neither authoritatively confirm nor correct any of our moral judgments: see *Authority in Morals* (London: Heythrop Monographs 1978) i–vii, 1–25; similarly Fuchs, *Christian Morality*, 6–7. On Hughes's argument, see John Finnis, "Reflections on an Essay in Christian Ethics . . ." *Clergy Review* 65 (1980) 51–57.

absolutes (of which the norm about contraception is but one) is false.

Thus, some argued that specific moral absolutes were proposed in the tradition, and can only be proposed, on the basis of a fallacious inference. Versions of the supposed fallacy vary widely. Some, like Joseph Fuchs, S.J., say that the tradition rests on the "naturalistic fallacy," which he explains as the fallacious inference from the natural givenness, facticity, *Gegebenheit*, of particular human faculties such as speech, to norms protecting their finalities.[19] Others, including some proportionalists, disagree.[20] Certainly Aquinas' explanation of practical principles, resumed and extended in this book, emphasizes strongly that these principles are not deduced from any facts, but are *per se nota*, self-evident. That is to say, they are the articulation of an understanding supervening on the experience of one's pre-rational inclinations but itself original and unmediated by any middle terms.[21] Again, his explanation of the morality of acts (see III.3) emphasizes that for moral purposes acts are specified and judged by reference, not to behavior's natural facticity, but to the object shaped by the acting person's intelligence and will. And this practical understanding and intending of objects is measured only by principles which ensure that the person is not deflected by feelings from an unrestrictedly reasonable service, not of faculties or their finalities as such but of the basic aspects of human fulfillment.

Other versions of the supposed fallacious inference identify it as the inference from God's creative will to his moral will,[22] or

19. Josef Fuchs, S.J., "Naturrecht oder naturalistischer Fehlschluss?" *Stimmen der Zeit* 29 (1988) 406–23; also *Christian Morality* 16–17.

20. As Richard McCormick said in 1978: "I do not see the service to moral science to volunteer . . . that all deontologists are at root physicalists or are guilty of a naturalistic fallacy. Some may be." *Notes . . . 1965 through 1980* 709.

21. See Finnis, *Natural Law and Natural Rights* chap. 2; John Finnis and Germain Grisez, "The Basic Principles of Natural Law: A Reply to Ralph McInerny," *American Journal of Jurisprudence* 26 (1981) 21 at 21–25.

22. See, e.g., Fuchs, *Christian Ethics in a Secular Arena* 78; Louis Janssens, "Norms and Priorities in a Love Ethic," *Louvain Studies* 6 (1977) 207 at 233, 236-37; James J. Walter, "Response to John Finnis: "A Theological Critique," in Thomas G. Fuechtmann, ed., *The Consistent Ethic of Life* (Kansas City: Sheed & Ward, 1988) 184-86; McCormick, *Notes . . . 1981 through 1984* 5 n. 13.

from intention to cause physical evil to intention to cause moral evil.[23] But those who defend the specific moral norms proposed by the tradition need not, should not, and customarily do not rely on any appeal to God's "will" to make clear either the content or the truth of those norms. And if intention to cause physical evil is understood to mean intention to destroy, damage or impede a basic human good as instantiated or instantiatable in the life of a particular human being or beings, then it is justifiable to conclude that that intention is morally evil. For: one adopting such an intention could not have a will compatible with integral human fulfillment, since no reason to do such harm could outweigh the reason not to do it (II.6).

Then again: Some say that the exceptionless norms proposed in the tradition irrationally abstract *some* elements from the total reality of a human action. They are not trying to revive the "Birth-Control Commission" theory. Rather, they contend that an action can rationally be evaluated as right or wrong only as a total state of affairs which includes all the circumstances and motivations, considered in relation to *all* the premoral but morally relevant goods and bads involved in that (envisaged) totality.[24]

When asked what one should be looking for when considering this vast array of circumstances and motivations and outcomes and goods and bads involved in them, answers have varied. An early offer was Joseph Fuchs's: behavior which will further humankind's self-realization and self-development overall and in the long run. An option experimented with by Louis Janssens, Peter Knauer, and Richard McCormick has not fared well: behavior which will not, in the long run, "undermine," "negate," or "contradict" the value directly sought in the behav-

---

23. E.g. Peter Knauer, S.J., "The Hermeneutic Function of the Principle of Double Effect," in Curran and McCormick, *Readings in Moral Theology* at 31-32.

24. E.g., Louis Janssens, "Ontic Evil and Moral Evil," *Louvain Studies* 4 (1972) 115 at 144 (also in Curran and McCormick, *Readings in Moral Theology* No. 1 40 at 73); Janssens, "Norms and Priorities in a Love Ethic," *Louvain Studies* 6 (1977) 207 at 231; McCormick, *Notes . . . 1965 through 1980* 701; Edward Vacek, S.J., "Proportionalism: One View of the Debate," *Theological Studies* 46 (1985) 287 at 313; Mahoney, *Making of Moral Theology* 309-21.

ior itself.[25] Recently a prudent caution has prevailed. So Edward Vacek laments, "*P* [proportionalism]—to its detriment—continues to use metaphors that imply a quantitative enterprise, but at bottom it demands a qualitative sensitivity to the depth and breadth [!] of value." Since he is unable to keep the quantitative metaphors out of even that sentence itself, no one will be surprised to see that the criterion he offers in the same paragraph is similarly simply quantitative in its formulation: "an increase of the good and a decrease of the bad."[26]

Thus, after fifteen years of energetic collaborative work, no progress has been made on McCormick's simple statement of 1973: In conflict situations, we should choose the lesser evil; "this statement is, it would seem, beyond debate; for the only alternative is that in conflict situations we should choose the greater evil, which is patently absurd."[27] The statement, of course, proved eminently debatable. The debate, however, proved to be brief. For it is demonstrable that McCormick's statement involves the simple logical fallacy of assuming that nonexhaustive alternatives are exhaustive. Indeed, as I and many others have argued, the alternatives ("greater good" and "lesser evil" identifiable by reason and prior to moral judgment) are not even available when the situation involves a rationally motivated, morally significant choice. So such choices must be guided by moral principles such as exclude unfairness, intention to harm or impede basic human goods, or other immoral motivations (III.6).

And these principles must all be satisfied if the action is to be right, morally good. As soon as one can see that an option fails one of the moral tests, one knows that that option is wrong. To

25. E.g., Janssens, "Ontic Evil and Moral Evil" 144; for critique of McCormick's version see John Finnis, *Fundamentals of Ethics*, (Oxford: Clarendon Press; Washington, D.C.: Georgetown University Press, 1983) 99–104; Brian V. Johnstone, "The Meaning of Proportionate Reason in Contemporary Moral Theology," *The Thomist* 49 (1985) 223–47.

26. "Proportionalism: One View of the Debate" 303.

27. Richard McCormick, S.J., "Ambiguity in Moral Choice" in Richard McCormick, S.J., and Paul Ramsey, eds., *Doing Evil to Achieve Good* (Chicago: Loyola University Press, 1978) 38.

go on examining the other aspects of the option is then mere distraction. Indeed, it is merely to torment oneself with temptation. In reality, the injunction to consider all the goods and bads in the totality of the situation, when there is no rational criterion for processing all the information, cannot (for all its authors' good intentions) be other than an invitation to devise rationalizations for doing what one feels like.

This conclusion is not disturbed by the proportionalists' frequently repeated but rarely if ever elaborated response: Surely, they say, the weighing and identification of greater premoral good or lesser evil, prior to (and for the purpose of guiding) choice, *must* be possible, since the tradition itself used a requirement and criterion of proportionality when it expounded and applied the "doctrine of double effect," the standard explanation of how causing bad side effects can be right.[28] But they are mistaken. The requirement of "proportionateness" proposed by Aquinas at the origin of the "doctrine"[29] used no concept of greater good or lesser evil and involved no scrutiny of overall net consequences; it merely required that the action which causes the foreseen harm must be no more harmful than is necessary for defending oneself then and there: the act must be *proportionatus fini*, proportioned to its own end.[30] When the Salmanticenses, in the midseventeenth century, generalized St. Thomas' discussion, they proposed that causing the unintended but foreseen and harmful side effect is morally upright only when one is "morally powerless to prevent it," bearing in mind "the specific character of the virtues to which the evil permitted is opposed."[31] Their criterion of the proportionality of the side effects was thus distinct, in principle, from an aggregation of premoral goods.

---

28. E.g., Fuchs, *Christian Morality* 16.
29. In *Summa Theol.* 2-2 q.64 a.7 (on lethal measures of self-defense).
30. Finnis, *Fundamentals of Ethics* 85.
31. Salmanticenses, *Cursus Theologicus*, vol. 7 *De Vitiis et Peccatis* (1647) tr. 13 disp. 10 dub. 6 nn. 244, 247 (where the authors add, "No utility, however great, will suffice [neque sufficit sola utilitas, quantumvis maxima]"); cf. J. T. Mangan, "An Historical Analysis of the Principle of Double Effect," *Theol. St.* 10 (1949) 40 at 57.

Similarly, when Joannes Gury, S.J., in 1850 stabilized the text-book tradition of what thereafter became known as the "doctrine" of double effect, he gave a similar explanation: there is a "proportionately serious reason for actuating the cause" of the harmful side effect, when "the author of the action would not be obliged by any virtue, e.g. from justice or charity, to omit the action."[32] Thus moral norms were conceived as controlling, not controlled by, any assessing of consequences. (This is no surprise, since the other requirements specified in the "doctrine" of double effect likewise propose moral limits on the pursuit of good consequences, limits such as lead proportionalists generally to reject the "doctrine.") In short: the claim that proportionalism simply generalizes a principle or method proposed by the tradition is historically erroneous.[33]

Then again: Some content themselves with saying that to propose specific moral absolutes is falsely to absolutize various criteria which, in a sound ethics or theology, would be subordi-

32. J. P. Gury, *Compendium Theologiae Moralis*, vol. 1 ([1850] 5th ed., Ratisbon, 1874), "de actibus humanis" c.2 n.9; see Mangan, "Historical Analysis" 60–61.

33. It may be helpful to add a note on the theological tradition concerning the question, Is it right to counsel the lesser evil? E. T. Hannigan, S.J., "Is It Ever Lawful to Advise the Lesser of Two Evils?" *Gregorianum* 30 (1949) 104–29, summarizes the results of a survey of a hundred theologians who wrote between Cajetan (at the beginning of the sixteenth century) and the mid-twentieth century. All these authors accepted without question that one may not do evil (here understood as commit a moral evil, sin) even for the sake of avoiding or preventing a greater evil (here understood, again, as a moral evil, a sin), and that therefore one may not choose to induce or advise another to commit one sin in order to distract him from committing a more serious sin. All agree that one may give advice whose meaning if not articulation is of the form, Don't have extramarital intercourse, but if you're determined to, at least make it fornication, not adultery (which adds injustice to the unchastity). But some (indeed many) thought it possible to extend advice of that form to advice of the form, If you are intent on doing some wrong such as murder, I suggest that you instead do some less serious wrong such as getting drunk. However, those who held this view defended it on the ground that such advice did not involve counseling, seeking, or inducing the choice of (moral) evil. Others judged (reasonably) that this defense rested on a faulty analysis of intention, action, and advice: see the strong historical review and critique in L. Bender, O.P., "Consulere minus malum," *Ephemerides Theologicae Lovanienses* 8 (1931) 592–614. But it is clear that the whole debate involved no challenge directed against any of the positions defended in this book.

nated to a single last end (such as reverence for God, accomplishment of his plan, and/or human salvation). Such an objection[34] simply begs the question. For the tradition, rightly understood, proposes that every exceptionless moral norm is subordinated to the supreme principles of morality: love and reverence for God and conformity to reason (which discloses to us something of the mind of God). The specific moral norms are proposed precisely as specifications of, implications of, love of God and of every human person made in his image.[35]

Similar to the last-mentioned argument is another, more popular argument: The moral absolutes falsely absolutize the human goods which they are claimed to protect. Every human good, however basic, is premoral, conditioned, created, limited, and, in sum, nonabsolute. Therefore no norm protecting such a good can be absolute.[36]

This argument, too, cannot survive, since it merely equivocates on the term "absolute." "Absolute moral norm" means no more than "exceptionless moral norm." Such norms are proposed as true, not because the goods they protect are absolute goods, but because it *cannot* be reasonable to have certain attitudes of will toward them, for instance, to intend to destroy, damage, or impede them.[37] The claim that such attitudes of will *can* be reasonable needs to be defended; the usual, proportionalist defense has proved rationally unsustainable (II.3).

Indeed, when we survey the two decades since 1968, we can

34. Advanced in 1988 by Karl Peschke as the decisive objection to the tradition: "Tragfähigkeit und Grenzen des Prinzips der Doppelwirkung," *Studia Moralia* 26 (1988) 101.

35. See John Finnis, Joseph Boyle, and Germain Grisez, *Nuclear Deterrence, Morality and Realism* (Oxford and New York: Clarendon Press, 1987) 283–94.

36. E.g., Franz Boeckle, *Fundamental Moral Theology* (New York: Pueblo, 1980) 236-37; McCormick, *Notes . . . 1965 through 1980* 709; Fuchs, *Personal Responsibility and Christian Morality*, (Washington, D.C.: Georgetown University Press; Dublin: Gill & Macmillan, 1983) 142, 212.

37. Consistently with the account developed in this book, Paul VI says in *Evangelii Nuntiandi* 8 (*Acta Apostolicae Sedis* 68 [1976] 10): "The Kingdom of God is to be considered, therefore, as the absolute good so that everything else is subordinate to it." The human goods of truth, life, justice, love, peace, and so on, stand to the Kingdom as parts to whole: see I.3, I.5, I.8, III.3, III.6.

see that the appeal to reason against the moral absolutes, an appeal which is still advertised in programmatic essays on the relations between "faith" and "reason," turns out, under the pressure of rational arguments, to be an appeal not to reason but to some intuitive process which is "beyond reduction to reasoning processes or analytic judgments"[38] and which is therefore fittingly called by those who rely on it an "instinct."[39] Karl Rahner, after he had abandoned the traditional view of specific moral absolutes which he had earlier expounded with memorable force,[40] spoke of a "faith instinct" in relation to problems of moral judgment;[41] but followers such as Fuchs and McCormick find an instinct which contradicts and thereby discredits the faith, or at least some of the constant and most firm teachings, of the church. In the pages to which they appeal, Rahner had seemed to equate this "faith instinct" with sheer will, operating without or beyond reason. Thus he said that genetic manipulation is to be opposed as immoral because "we do not *want*

38. McCormick, *Doing Evil to Achieve Good* 250. Bernard Hoose, *Proportionalism: The American Debate and Its European Roots* (Washington, D.C.: Georgetown University Press, 1987), admits (89) that proportionalists have no method but absurdly persists in claiming (95) that proportionalists reach their conclusions by "calculations." His central confusion is to suppose (89) that if any comparisons of value (e.g., human beings are more valuable than stones) can be made, it must be possible to make proportionalist comparisons of the premoral goods and bads involved in *options* for morally significant choice. Non sequitur. Hoose's case for proportionalism seems to rest on his intuition that one must be able to "tell a little untruth," i.e., lie, in certain emergencies (73–74, 93, 95), and this in turn seems connected with his assumption (74) that if one may not lie, one must tell the truth. He refrains from testing his intuition against St. Augustine's counterarguments.

39. Ibid. 251. See also McCormick, *Notes . . . 1981 through 1984* 16: "actions where we sense very strongly (sense of profanation, outrage, intuition) that the actions are counterproductive [in general and in the long run]."

40. See Karl Rahner, *Nature and Grace* (London and New York: Sheed & Ward, 1963) 96–106 (a critique of situation ethics originally published in 1949 and republished by him in German in 1957).

41. Karl Rahner, S.J., *Theological Investigations*, vol. 9 (New York: Crossroad, 1976) 243; McCormick, *Doing Evil* 250–51; Fuchs, *Personal Responsibility and Christian Morality* 122. See Germain Grisez, *The Way of the Lord Jesus*, vol. 1 *Christian Moral Principles* (Chicago: Franciscan Herald Press, 1983) 159, 169–70; Grisez, "Moral Absolutes: A Critique of the View of Josef Fuchs, S.J.," *Anthropotes* 1985/2 155 at 182.

to manipulate"; our "'instinct' justifiably has the courage to say *Stat pro ratione voluntas* [will fills the gap where reason runs out] because such a confession need not be overcautious about making a decision."[42] If we follow Rahner's statement as closely as it will bear, we may find in it some confirmation for the hypothesis that, underlying the whole effort to develop a theoretical critique of the tradition's absolutes is a simple *antecedent* wish to approve some of the actions they exclude.

4. Prudence misconceived: the absolutes aesthetically dissolved

I have been reviewing the most representative instances of one genre of arguments against the moral absolutes of the tradition. Arguments of this genre all take ethics to be a *techne*, a technique of producing a desirable state of affairs presupposed to be the goal of action. All such arguments collapse, for a reason inferable from the classical thesis that there is a significant difference between ethics and *techne*: The end of human existence is not a goal producible by human artifice; it simply lacks the *particularity* of a determinate objective. Without that particularity or determinacy, one simply cannot make the comparisons which constitute a technique: "this is the way . . . and that is not the way . . . to . . ."; "this is more effective than that. . . ." The basic aspects of human fulfillment, even in one person's existence and possibilities, are open-ended, and as possibilities of fulfillment for all persons and communities they are all the more open-ended, all the more irreducible to any producible goal. The upshot is an appeal to "instinct," "sense" or "intuition."

But not all critiques of moral absolutes follow proportionalism in reducing ethics to a grandiose technique for improving "the human condition." Some critiques follow another model, often based on a certain reading of Aristotle's discussions of prudence, *phronesis*, practical wisdom or reasonableness. But

42. Rahner, *Thedogical Investigations*, vol. 9, at 251.

underpinning this model is perhaps another reduction of ethics—not to a technique so much as to something like a creative fine art. And the upshot is, again, an appeal to "intuition."

In the mastery of matter to make an object more or less for its own sake, whether it be a poem, a sentence of a lecture, a dance, a painting, a novel, or whatever, the maker is not guided by any goal adequately identifiable independently of the efficacious means which the maker might calculate and adopt for achieving it. Thus, artistic creation outruns technique. Instead, such makers, responding to the sensible particularity of the matter on or with which they work, are each guided by a "sense" of the object, a sense which cannot be articulated otherwise than by producing the object, yet which somehow serves to measure the adequacy of any particular attempt. There is interaction between the process of creation and this imaginative "conception" or "intuition" or "anticipation" of the object; the anticipation may be refined and altered, even radically, without however disappearing, during the process. To assess the artistic, aesthetic worth (goodness or badness) of the final product involves an aesthetic appreciation of the unity between "what the work is trying to say" and "how the work is saying it"; the aesthetic understanding does not come to rest at either pole; nor does it use criteria wholly prior and external to the composition itself. Provided the composition has a kind of inner unity, clarity, integrity, it can have an aesthetic worth which can govern and reshape, rather than be governed by, preexisting standards generalizing the features of previous aesthetic objects which by their own inner unity, clarity, integrity established *for themselves* their artistic worth.

Some conceive the moral life in a fashion analogous to this. They see moral actions as prior to moral principles and norms, which are but the "public distillation" of morally good action. They deny that it is possible to find criteria or methods of reasoning which could enable one "abstractly to recognize what is right." Rather, the actions of "the virtuous agent" simply show the excellence that is possible in human behavior, "just as a

superior athlete shows what can be done in a particular game."
They propose that thinking about a situation which calls for
something to be done "is not the consideration of maxims and
the placing of a case under a general rule." They claim that
moral principles and norms form no kind of system; none of
them has its truth by being derivable from or otherwise related
to the others; each has its truth "by living off what [virtuous and
vicious] agents do."[43]

Though it is often left unstated, the conclusion seems clear:
The wrongness of certain choices cannot be known in advance;
one cannot understand norms as having their truth by participat-
ing in reason's principled directiveness toward an ideal which,
though not attainable by human artifice, nonetheless makes possible a critique of every choice which, at the behest of feelings,
would cut back on reason (that is, on service to all aspects of
integral human fulfillment). In other words, the aesthetic-
prudential conception of virtuous choice and action denies that
the tradition's specific moral norms truly identify types of act
incompatible with love of God and neighbor, and with seeking
first the Kingdom.

Accordingly, some have justified rejection of the norm about
contraception, and of other norms they find unconvincing,
by appealing simply to an "incommunicable wisdom" of "prudence," which "sees" (to use Aristotle's word) the right choice

43. See Robert Sokolowski, *Moral Action* (Bloomington: Indiana University
Press, 1985) 152; *The God of Faith and Reason* (Notre Dame, Ind.: Notre Dame
University Press, 1982) 62–63. For another version: Walter E. Conn, *Conscience:
Development and Self-Transcendence* (Birmingham, Ala.: Religious Education
Press, 1981) 209–10: "an ethics grounded in an understanding of conscience as
self-transcending subjectivity" can perhaps "best be compared to literary (or
music . . .) criticism and aesthetics. . . ." "The ethical critic, as he or she attempts
to understand and shed some light on a problem like abortion, works in the light of
the theoretical principles of foundational ethics, but does not use these principles
as premises from which to deduce answers to particular problems, any more than
the literary critic deduces an interpretation of a poem from aesthetic principles. . . . Further, because the ethical analyst realizes that decisions are made
in particular situations according to the subject's best *creative* understanding of
the complex concreteness of the situation, he or she does not regard interpreta-
tions of general problem areas like abortion as applicable in a *deductive* way to
particular cases. . . ."

but only "in the situation," conceived as a field free from rational and therefore articulable criteria, that is, from *applicable* standards for identifying which choices are not right. Notice, they are not contending that the choosing escapes moral judgment, as right or wrong. But they conceive such judgment on something like the aesthetic model I have described.

Thus they overlook the profound difference between the open-ended goods of persons, which are the intelligible subject matter of moral action, and the *material* on which every fine art works. Moral deliberation is about intelligibles from beginning to end; it moves not from the general to the particular but from the general to the specific. In an art, features of a particular item of matter can make a significant difference to the artist's performance, a difference controlled by the artist's imagination and other nonintellectual sensitivities and acts.

And all these accounts overlook the difference between norms which direct one away from wrong choice and norms whose directiveness is affirmative. In relation to all the latter, but not all the former, what these theorists say of all norms indiscriminately has some truth (even if it is still not the whole truth). When the question is what *should* be done, the (affirmative) norms themselves, however specific, leave something, often much, to be settled by a conscience which now must be measured by the unintelligible particularity of one's own feelings, by an intuitional grip, by the "discernment" which constitutes a particular prudence, about what is to be done. Yet there remain some factors which make choices always wrong, and which in their bearing on specific types of act can be described with sufficient specificity to leave no room for any intuition of feelings which could or need be ordered by a virtue of prudence.

The true virtue of prudence, as explained by the great masters of the tradition such as St. Thomas Aquinas, will certainly supplement deduction from principles with a sensitive discernment. But prior to this perfecting of deliberation by prudential judgment, the virtue of prudence will have played its other essential role: of excluding from deliberation all options which involve the violation of specific moral norms and are therefore unjust or unchaste or in other ways disrespectful of basic human good(s) immediately at stake in possible options. The prudent person does not deliberate about whether to commit adultery, to what extent, with whom, on what occasions.

Here the "prudentialist" intuitionist, or "situation ethicians"—whose views seem substantially identical to those condemned in 1956 by the Holy See[44]—may well object: Surely the factors which usually make an option wrong cannot make it wrong in a situation in which there are such-and-such other, exceptional factors? But, one must ask, what is it about these other factors that makes the act right? Well, surely they—outweigh the "wrong-making" factors! Alas, we have been here before: intuitionism has turned into an ad hoc proportionalism before our eyes, with all the attendant burdens of incoherence (II.3–5).

5. A summary conclusion

Does the Christian belief in moral absolutes replicate the Stoic slogan, "Fiat justitia, ruat coelum" ("Let right be done, though the heavens fall")?

By no means. The Stoic cosmology did not, in fact, allow for any collapse of the heavens. Christian understanding of the divine plan envisages that the heavens *will* someday fall. But not that they will fall because right is done. This world's need for re-

44. See "Instructio S. Officii de ethica situationis," *Acta Apostolicae Sedis* 48 (1956) 144–45; *Denz.-Schoen.* 3918–21; see also Pius XII, Address to Young Catholic Women, 18 April 1952, *Acta Apostolicae Sedis* 44 (1952) 413–19. However, it is not only the prudentialists who espouse an ethic practically indistinguishable from that condemned in 1956. A reading of Josef Fuchs, S.J., "Morale théologique et morale de situation," *Nouvelle Revue Théologique* 76 (1954) 1073–85; "Ethique objective et éthique de situation," *Nouvelle Revue Théologique* 78 (1956) 798–818; and *Natural Law* ([German original 1952] Dublin: Gill, 1965) esp. 90–92, makes clear that this influential theologian's understanding of the tradition was always hospitable to both prudentialist and proportionalist transformations of the tradition, and that his adoption of proportionalism during the period of the Birth-Control Commission was by no means the revolution in his own thought that it is often taken to have been.

creation stems not from the doing of justice and right, but from sin. And the Christian faith proposes that doing the right is redemptive: that, indeed, it sets the stage for the new heavens and the new earth. For, in union with Jesus' acceptance of death, a doing of the right merits the raising up of the rest of the universe, a raising up already begun with the resurrection of Jesus, so that the choice and doing of right will be found again in the completed Kingdom.

Moral action, then, is cooperation with the carrying out of God's plan. The rationale of moral action, including adherence to the moral absolutes, is the ideal of integral human fulfillment, an ideal which Christian faith transforms into the hope for the Kingdom as it will be. To turn away from the moral norms which God has made knowable by reason and confirmed by the Gospel, on the plea that they do not make sense, is to forget that what makes sense in the construction of even a human city or building is discernible only to those who can envisage the whole project.

The martyrs of every age have acted in the consciousness that this world, too, has an architect. They have understood that creation's unfolding is shaped by an all-encompassing plan of divine wisdom, in which every person's destiny finds its full sense only in the destiny of the whole universe, yet every person is created and sustained for his or her own sake. They have accepted that to respect the moral limits proposed by the creator as implicit in his creative wisdom is, therefore, supremely intelligent and reasonable—is to do all that in this life we can do towards enhancing good and lessening evil, on the whole and in the long run.

Index

Abelard, Peter, 65
abortion, 3, 9, 13n, 17, 27, 67, 85, 90n, 103n
absolute, absoluteness: of certain moral norms, 2–3, 99; of God, 3; "false absolutizing," 46, 98–99
absolutes: specific moral, 4, 6, 11, 94; artificially constructed, 4; "formal," 4, 37; implication of principle excluding doing evil for good, 81; "practical," 5n; protect basic human goods, 24; requirements of reason, 29, 40–47; "transcendental," 6n
acceptance, not intention, 60, 68–69, 106
act, action, acts: ambiguity of all action-related terms, 72; "base," 33–35; -description, 68–70; evaluation only "as a totality," 16–17, 20, 89, 93, 95; "exterior" v. "interior," 66; intransitive effects of, 73n; intransitivity of, 20; intrinsically wrong, 2, 38n, 66, 76n; per se (in themselves) wrong, 2, 66; physical, 39; reflexive aspects of, 21, 22; specified by intention/object, 69–70, 94; wrong by reason of object, 2, 38
adultery: conjugal intercourse compared, 38; defined, 8, 36, 65; definition of marriage, and, 28; "necessity," and, 33–36, 65; "right time for," never, 32, 105; wrongness of (not by definition), 3, 6–9, 35, 37; other references, 27, 98n
aesthetic appreciation, 102
affirmative norms/precepts, 28, 91, 104
"agent-centered" moral norms, 50
Albert the Great, St., 32, 34, 35, 62, 90
Ambrose, St., 86n
amputation, 78–79
analogia fidei, 7n

"antinomianism," 61
Aristotle: on involuntariness, 33; on moral absolutes, 31–34, 36; on prudence (practical reasonableness), 101, 103; on reflexivity of action, 22; other references, 51, 75
art, 102–3
Aspasius, 33
Augustine of Hippo, St.: on doing evil for sake of good, 62–65; on lying, 63–65; on permissive v. intending will, 77n; on suicide, 60n; other references, 11, 27, 44, 66

babies, making of, 3, 6, 26–27, 85
backsliding, 52
"balance of goods," 24
Balthasar, Hans Urs von, 8n
Bay, Michael du, 23n
behavior, stipulatively distinguished from action, 26, 37–40, 43, 65, 66, 70–72, 94
Bentham, Jeremy, 13, 23, 30
Bender, L., O.P., 98n
Bible: Exodus 20:12–17, 11n; Deuteronomy 5:16–21, 11n; 30:19, 22; Sirach 15:11–20, 22; Wisdom 15:1–2, 62n; Matthew 5:17–28, 7; 19, 59; 19:4–9, 7n; 19:16–19, 7; 19:19, 7; 22:36–49; Mark 10, 59n; 10:4–12, 7n; 10:17–19, 7; Luke 16, 59n; 16:18–20, 7, 7n; 18, 59n; John 5:40, 15n; 13:37, 60; 15:13, 60; 18:4, 60; 18:37, 60; 19:11, 60; Romans 1:23–31, 7; 2:14–15, 7; 3:5–8, 60–63, 67n, 74; 3:8, 28n, 36, 60–63, 71; 3, 15; 6:1 & 15, 60; 6, 15; 3:8–10, 7; 1 Corinthians, 8n
Black, Matthew, 61n
blasphemy, 8, 65
Boeckle, Franz, 99n; of cities, 3, 25, 67; of military v. "military" targets, 68

107

merit, 106
moral absolutes, *see* absolutes
morality: first principle of, 45; fundamentals, 1
moral falsities, 45
moral principles and norms: absolute, 1–3, 46; inevitable limits and, 71; non-absolute, 1; "material" ("physical") v. "formal," 5–6, 10n, 37–40; specifications of love of God and human persons, 99; "transcendental," 6n; as truths, 1, 4, 11, 30; "valid only generally" only a generalization, 90–91; "untrue," 11n
More, St. Thomas, 9, 50
murder: choosing death as a means, 70; exceptionlessly wrong, 47; not "wrong by definition," 31–32, 35–37; "better do one than fail to stop ten," 49–50; other reference, 98n

Nagasaki, 18, 19
Nagel, Thomas, 49n
"Natural Family Planning" (NFP), 86
natural law, 7, 9, 25, 93n
nature, human: and artifice, 87; (un)changeability, 24–28; known partly by practical knowledge of human fulfilment, 25, 29, 42
Nazi genocide, 25
negative norms/precepts, 27–30, 91, 104–5
New Testament, 6, 27
noncombatants, 25n, 68
normativity, moral 40–41

object of acts, 38, 39n, 94; defined, 69–70
O'Connell, Timothy E., 23n
Old Scholiast, 34–36
Old Testament, 6, 28, 38n
Origen, 76n

pain, sensory evil, intelligible good, 79
pain-killing drugs, 39
parenesis, 8; v. instruction, 7
Parfit, Derek, 21
pastoral considerations, 30, 87

Paul, St., 8, 9, 11, 15, 27; on doing evil for sake of good, 60–63
per se, 2, 9, 74–75
perverted faculty argument(s), 87, 94
Paul VI, Pope, 2n, 40n, 45n, 62, 99n; "Birth Control Commission," 88n, 89n, 93, 95, 105n
Peschke, K.-H., S.V.D., 46n, 77n, 98n
Philo Judaeus, 77
Pius V, Pope, 23n
Pius XI, Pope, 62
Pius XII, Pope, 9n, 40n, 56n, 105n
Plato, 27, 48, 51, 54
persons, reality of, 58; *see also* love
practical knowledge, 44–45n
practical principles, 55, 94
preference, desire and reason, 55
progress, *see* historicity
"proportionalism," 14–16, 19–24; admissions of lack of rational method, 100–101; "absolute against causing moral evil," 48–49, 75–76; adultery and, 36; common speech and, 54; confusion of intention and cause, 77; defined, 90; implicit, of ancients, 35; incoherent with rationally motivated free choice, 51–54, 96–97, 105; inconsistent with doctrine of divine providence, 15–20, 62; and instinct, 100; lying and, 100n; and "principle of double effect," 98; quantitative character of, 96; selfish motivation and, 52; and Socratic dictum, 47–51; and directly willing (intending) pre-moral evils, 75–76, 95; other references, 94
"proportionality," 97–98
"proportionate reason," 8
proposal for choice and action, 40, 68–73
Protestantism, 15
providence: divine, 12–16, 67, 76; human, 13, 19
prudence, 82–83, 101–5
punishment, 79–81

rape, 39n
Rahner, Karl, S.J., 24–25, 100–101
rationalization, 44, 63n, 69, 97

Ratzinger, Joseph Cardinal, 8n
reason, 29, 40–47; and mind of
God, 99; and service of integral
human fulfilment, 103; fettered v.
unfettered, 44–46; passions and,
44n, 81; against a basic reason,
against reason, 54–55, 95
Reconciliatio et Paenitentia, 2, 38, 69
reflexivity of choice, 20–24
religion: doing evil for sake of, 63n
religious freedom, 26
responsibility, 14–15; human or divine, 16, 63n; for side effects, 71
revelation, 6, 29, 30, 93n
revenge, 44, 46–47, 80, 81
Robinson, J. A. T., 61n, 62n
"rule v. value," 11

Salmanticenses (Discalced Carmelites
of Salamanca), 97
Sanday, William, 61n
Sanders, E. P., 61n
Scheffler, Samuel, 21n, 49n
Schoeps, H. J., 6n
Scholz, Franz, 32, 78n, 90, 92n
Schüller, Bruno, S.J., 17n, 32n, 47–
49, 75–76, 77n
Schürmann, H., 8n
secularism, 15n, 84–85, 88
Segundo, Juan Luis, S.J., 13n
self-defense and "self-defense," 39n;
deadly force and, 55–57, 78–79
self-destruction, 11
self-determination (creation of character), 58, 72
semper et ad semper v. *semper sed
non ad semper*, 28, 91
sex, 9, 10, 29, 37, 73, 85–86, 88–89
side effects, 64; "built-in," possible,
73; defined, 70–71; inevitability of
bad, 71; "proportionateness" of,
97–98; moral responsibility for,
71–72
situation ethics, 105; criticized by
early Rahner, 100
slavery, 26, 27, 85
Smart, J. J. C., 21n
Socrates, 27, 47, 49–50, 51, 54, 64n
Sokolowski, Robert, 103n
spanking children, 78–79
states of affairs, comparative evaluation of, 49–51, 53–54

sterilization, 40, 72
specific: judgments, as universals, 4n,
103–4; moral absolutes, 4, 6
Stagg, Frank, 61n
"stain of sin," 73n
Stoics, 105
Strauss, Leo, 6n
suicide, 9, 11, 27, 60, 67–68, 90n
Sullivan, Francis A., S.J., 92n
superior orders, plea of, 25

"tautologies," moral absolutes as
(not), 32, 36–37, 67n
technical thinking, 13, 20, 101
"teleology," 49
Ten Commandments, *see* Decalogue
theft, 27, 65
Theophilus of Antioch, St., 9n
Thirty Tyrants, 48, 50
Thomas Aquinas, St., 10n, 11, 15n,
27, 28, 39n; on adultery *pro utilitate* (overthrow of tyranny), 36; on
conjugal and adulterous intercourse, 38; on Aristotle on absolutes, 33; on *bonum ex integra
causa*, 17n; on capital punishment,
56; on direct v. indirect, 75n; on
divine "dispensations," 91; on
doing evil for sake of good, 56n,
62; on *finis operis;* on first practical
principles, 94; on free choice, 23n,
74; on God and permission of evil,
76, 77n; on "intention" v.
"choice," 70; on justification of
choice as "lesser evil," 56n; on
lying, 34, 67n; on means as ends,
69; on *per se* v. *praeter intentionem*, 75; on *per se nota* practical
principles, 94; on negative norms,
53n; on proportionate means, 97;
on prudence (practical reasonableness), 104; on retributive
punishment, 56n; on specification
and morality of acts, 94; *ut in
pluribus* v. *ut in paucioribus*, 90–
91; *via media* between Abelard and
Lombard, 66
transplantation, 79
transvesting, 33
Trent, Council of, 74–75
tyranny, 36; Socrates and, 48

Moral Absolutes was composed in Sabon by D&T
Typesetting, Nashville, Tennessee, and designed and
produced by Kachergis Book Design, Pittsboro,
North Carolina

Printed in the United States
201208BV00002B/1-234/A

9 780813 207452